The Gen X Series

IMO NSO NCO IEO

International Mathematics Olympiad | National Science Olympiad | National Cyber Olympiad | International English Olympiad

OLYMPIAD SAMPLE PAPERS 2

Useful for Olympiads Conducted at School, National & International Levels

Compiled By
Editorial Board

Strictly According to the Latest Syllabus of Olympiad

V&S PUBLISHERS

Published by:

V&S PUBLISHERS

F-2/16, Ansari road, Daryaganj, New Delhi-110002
☎ 23240026, 23240027 • *Fax:* 011-23240028
Email: info@vspublishers.com • *Website:* www.vspublishers.com

Regional Office : Hyderabad
5-1-707/1, Brij Bhawan (Beside Central Bank of India Lane)
Bank Street, Koti, Hyderabad - 500 095
☎ 040-24737290
E-mail: vspublishershyd@gmail.com

Branch Office : Mumbai
Jaywant Industrial Estate, 1st Floor–108, Tardeo Road
Opposite Sobo Central Mall, Mumbai – 400 034
☎ 022-23510736
E-mail: vspublishersmum@gmail.com

ISBN 978-93-579422-7-0
New Edition

DISCLAIMER

Publisher's Note

The current decade has firmly established V&S Publishers as one of the Leading Publishers of General Trade Mass Appeal Books across popular genres along with Academic Books for School Children. Having been in publishing trade for over 40 years, we understand the need of the hour when it comes to Books. After successfully publishing around 600 titles in the last decade and establishing a pan India network of booksellers & distributors including ecommerce platforms – Amazon, Flipkart etc; we determined after a nation-wide market research in tier 1, 2 and 3 cities that preparatory materials for status-acquiring OLYMPIAD BOOKS is the need of the hour.

And in true spirit, the Olympiad books on Science, Maths, English and Cyber published for classes 1 to 10 was picked by students off the shelf in no time. It acquired the 'Bestseller' image. Encouraged by this huge acceptability of our Olympiad Series among parents, students and booksellers alike, we at V&S Publishers decided to take PREPARATION to the next level by bringing out another handholding masterpiece – Olympiad Sample Papers.

These Sample Papers are the virtual replicas of the actual exam papers.

Yes! These Sample Papers are the virtual replicas of the actual exam papers. Inclusion of two sets each for Science, Maths, English and Cyber subjects from classes 1 to 10 in respective books are believed to be adequate to prepare students mentally for 'live exam conditions.' Anything else would have been 'under-preparation' or over-preparation'

You will hardly be able to differentiate the Sample Papers from the Actual Exam Papers. All this has been made possible by the people who have been in their respective fields for years – coaching and guiding students to succeed in this vital exam.

P.S. While every care has been taken to ensure correctness of content, if you come across any error, howsoever minor, anywhere in the book, do not hesitate to discuss with your teachers while pointing that out to us in no uncertain terms.

We wish you All the Best!

Contents

INTERNATIONAL MATHEMATICS OLYMPIAD (IMO)

Mock Test Paper 1

Total Questions : 35 | Time : 1 Hour

I M O
INTERNATIONAL MATHEMATICS OLYMPIAD

PATTERN AND MARKING SCHEME				
Section	**(1) Logical Reasoning**	**(2) Mathematical Reasoning**	**(3) Everyday Mathematics**	**(4) Achievers Section**
No. of Questions	10	10	10	5
Marks per Questions	1	1	1	2

SYLLABUS

Section – 1: Patterns, Odd One Out, Measuring Units, Geometrical Shapes, Analogy, Ranking Test, Grouping of Figures, Embedded Figures, Coding-Decoding.

Section – 2: Numerals, number names and Number Sense (3-Digit Numbers), Computation Operations, Length, Weight, Capacity, Time, Temperature, Money, Lines, Shapes and Solids, Pictographs, Patterns.

Section – 3: Syllabus as per Section– 2.

Section – 4: Higher Order Thinking Questions – Syllabus as per Section – 2.

LOGICAL REASONING

1. What will come next in the sequence on the compartment?

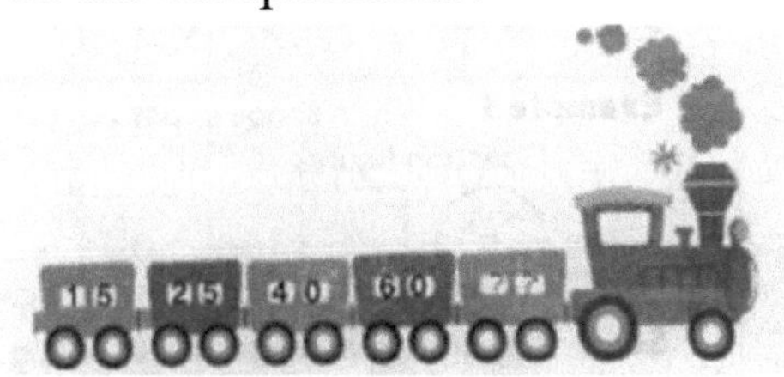

(A) 85 (B) 95
(C) 100 (D) 80

2. Count the number of straight lines in the given figure.

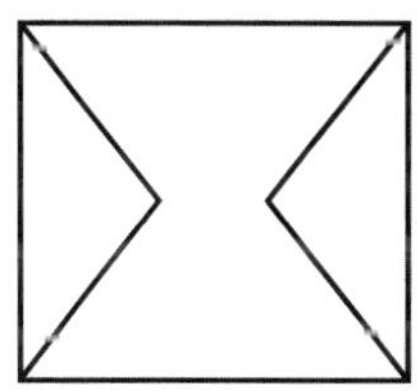

(A) 6 (B) 5
(C) 7 (D) 8

3. Complete the second pair in the same way as first pair.

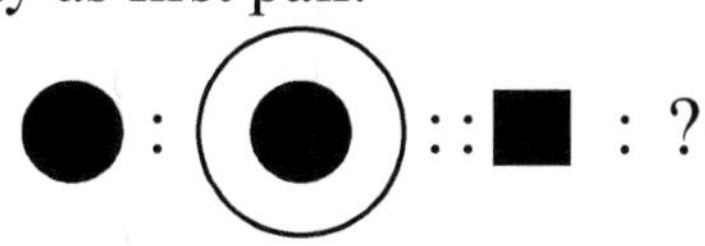

(A) 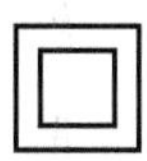 (B) 
(C)  (D) 

4. Which of the following toys is costlier?

(A) 

(B) 

(C) 

(D) 

5. Which shape or pattern belongs to the group of shapes given below?

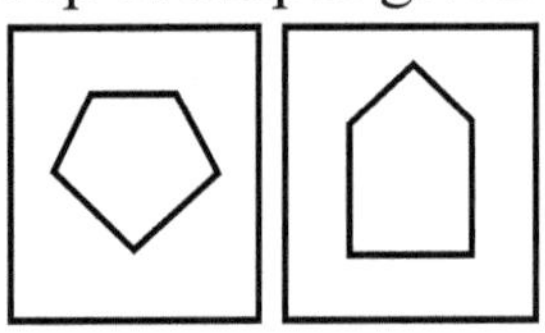

(A) 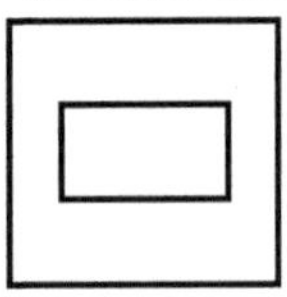

(B) 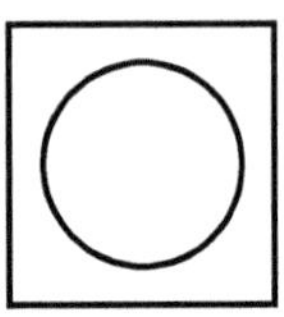

(C) 

(D) 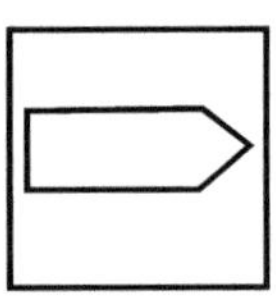

6. Choose the figure which will complete the following pattern.

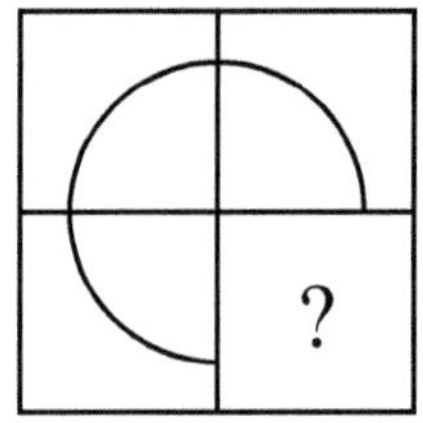

(A) 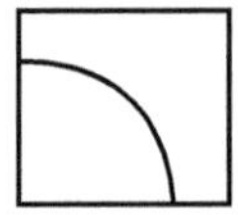　(B) 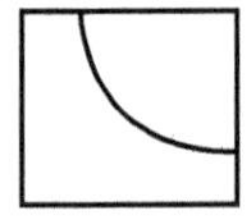

(C) 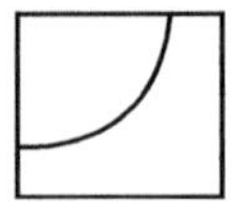　(D) 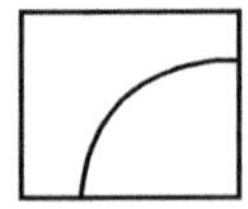

7. If PET is coded as TEP, then find the code for SET.

(A) TSE　(B) TES
(C) STA　(D) SAT

8. Three out of four figures form a group. Identify the figure that does not fit into the group.

(A) 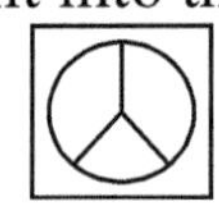　(B) 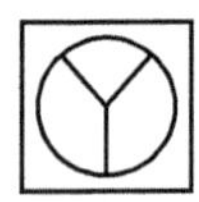

(C) 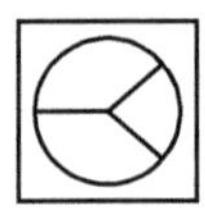　(D) 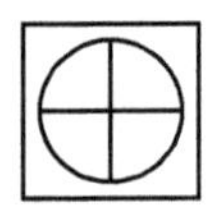

9. How many stairs are there between 5th stair and 12th stair?

(A) 8　(B) 7
(C) 6　(D) 5

10. Find the odd one out.

(A) 　(B) 

(C) 　(D) 

11. Which of the following is less than 700 by 25?
(A) 625 (B) 675
(C) 725 (D) 650

12. 8 × 7 is 29 more than which of the given numbers?
(A) 37 (B) 17
(C) 27 (D) 85

13. 36 lemon juice bottles are shared equally among 6 friends. How many bottles will each friend get?
(A) 10 (B) 5
(C) 6 (D) 4

14. In a leap year, how many days are there in the month of February?
(A) 29 (B) 28
(C) 31 (D) 30

15. Observe the given solid carefully and answer the given question.

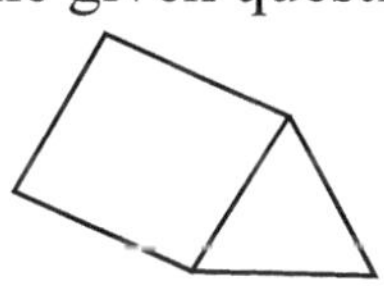

How many triangular faces does the solid have?
(A) 2 (B) 0
(C) 1 (D) 3

16. Study the picture carefully and answer the given question.

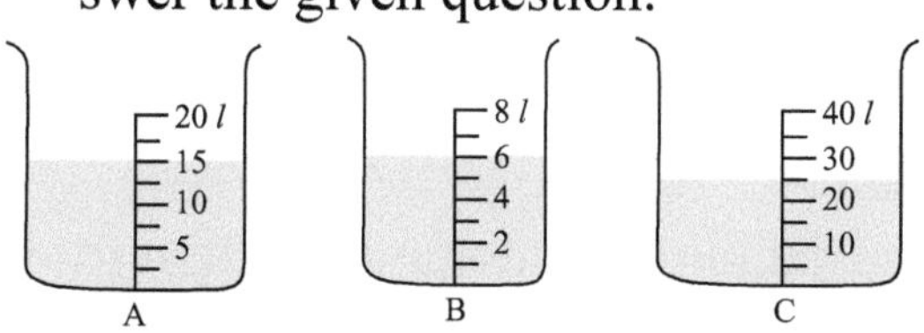

Which beaker holds the maximum amount of water?
(A) C
(B) B
(C) Both (A) and (C)
(D) A

17. What is the temperature shown by the thermometer ?

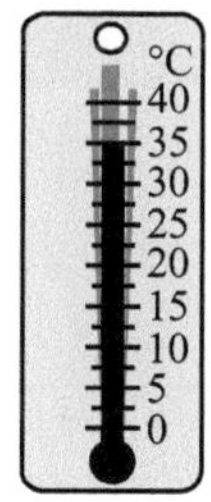

(A) 40° C (B) 35° C
(C) 30° C (D) 25° C

18. Which number can replace the question mark?

Before	Number	After
849	?	851

(A) 949 (B) 805
(C) 850 (D) 848

19. Tanya went to the supermarket where she bought 3 items. The items cost ₹ 80 in all.

Toy car	₹ 35
Story book	₹ 25
Pencil box	₹ 15
Water bottle	₹ 20

Which 3 items did she buy?
(A) 3 story books
(B) A toy car, a story book and a pencil box
(C) A toy car, a story book and a water bottle
(D) 3 water bottles and a story book

20. Look at the picture graph and answer the given question.

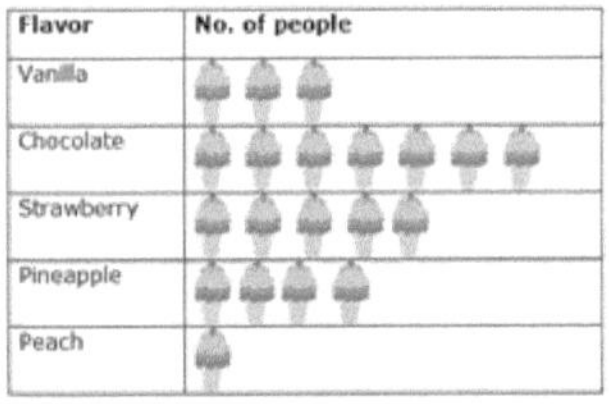

Which ice-cream flavor do you think is the most popular choice?

(A) Strawberry (B) Vanilla
(C) Chocolate (D) Pineapple

EVERYDAY MATHEMATICS

21. Ekta buys 25 water bottles for her sisters. Each girl gets 5 bottles. How many sisters does Ekta have?

(A) 10 (B) 4
(C) 5 (D) 9

22. Ritika had 1000 grams of rice. She sold 150 g on Monday and 200 g on Tuesday. How many grams of rice does she have now?

(A) 630 g (B) 520 g
(C) 650 g (D) 603 g

23. Priya bought the following items:

A pair of shoes cost ₹ 118 more than a scarf. How much she has to pay for all the items?

(A) ₹ 550 (B) ₹ 632
(C) ₹ 709 (D) ₹ 354

24. The given clocks show when Radhika, Vibha and Varsha started their guitar session on Saturday afternoon. Who started practice earliest?

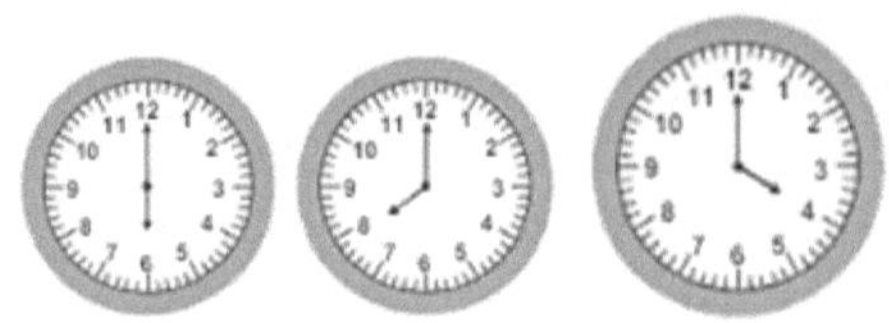

(A) Radhika
(B) Vibha and Radhika
(C) Varsha
(D) Varsha and Vibha

25. The following graph shows number of books sold by a bookseller in 4 different months. Study the graph and answer the following question.

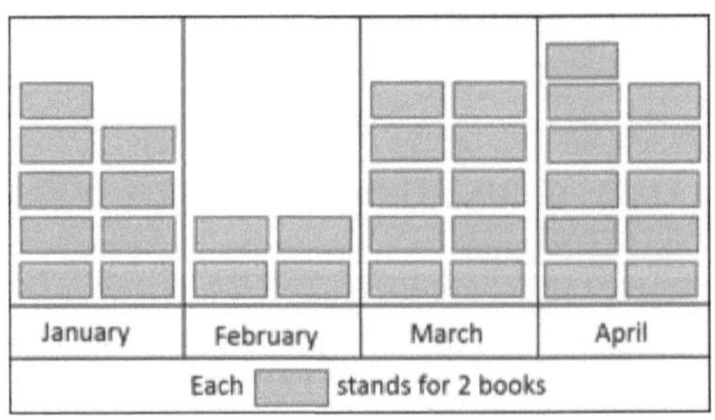

How many books were sold in month of January?

(A) 20 (B) 28
(C) 18 (D) 8

26. Nandini has to draw a pattern for her assignment. How many triangles does she need to draw the given pattern?

(A) 6 (B) 5
(C) 8 (D) 6

27. A group of students is holding an object in their hands having different numbers on it as shown below. Who is holding an object with an odd number?

(A) Pinky and Anu
(B) Madhu
(C) Pinky, Anu and Lalli
(D) Madhu and Pinky

28. Maria's plant is 6 cm taller than Mansi's plant. If height of Mansi's plant is 20 cm, what will be the height of Maria's plant.
(A) 28 cm (B) 26 cm
(C) 14 cm (D) 36 cm

29. Tina bought 12 notebooks. Each book had 40 pages. What is the total number of pages in all notebooks?
(A) 480 (B) 458
(C) 460 (D) 482

30. Anisha collected 28 stamps. Kanak collected 12 stamps more than Anisha. How many stamps did both of them collect?
(A) 35 (B) 50
(C) 68 (D) 42

ACHIEVERS SECTION

31. What time is it when it is three hours to12 midnight?
(A) 4 a.m. (B) 10 p.m.
(C) 9 p.m. (D) 3 a.m.

32. At 2:00, temperature was 40 degrees. At 4:00, temperature was 35 degrees. At 6:00, temperature was 30 degrees. What will be the temperature at 8:00, if the same pattern continues?
(A) 20 degrees (B) 15 degrees
(C) 25 degrees (D) 30 degrees

33. Tanya wants to paint her room so she bought 4 tins of oil paint. Each tin contains 2 L of paint. How much paint did she bought?
(A) 8 L (B) 10 L
(C) 12 L (D) 6 L

34. The total mass of 4 bananas and a bunch of strawberries is 860 g.The mass of each banana is 140 g .What is the mass of the bunch of strawberries?
(A) 320 g (B) 300 g
(C) 280 g (D) 340 g

35. Mahi bought a watch for ₹100. The watch costs 5 times as much as a cheaper watch. How much does the cheaper watch cost?

(A) ₹ 10
(B) ₹ 20
(C) ₹ 500
(D) ₹ 60

Mock Test Paper 2

I M O
INTERNATIONAL MATHEMATICS OLYMPIAD

Total Questions : 35 | Time : 1 Hour

PATTERN AND MARKING SCHEME				
Section	**(1) Logical Reasoning**	**(2) Mathematical Reasoning**	**(3) Everyday Mathematics**	**(4) Achievers Section**
No. of Questions	10	10	10	5
Marks per Questions	1	1	1	2

SYLLABUS

Section – 1: Patterns, Odd One Out, Measuring Units, Geometrical Shapes, Analogy, Ranking Test, Grouping of Figures, Embedded Figures, Coding-Decoding.

Section – 2: Numerals, number names and Number Sense (3-Digit Numbers), Computation Operations, Length, Weight, Capacity, Time, Temperature, Money, Lines, Shapes and Solids, Pictographs, Patterns.

Section – 3: Syllabus as per Section– 2.

Section – 4: Higher Order Thinking Questions – Syllabus as per Section – 2.

LOGICAL REASONING

1. Choose the figure which is different from others.

(A) 
(B) 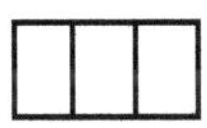
(C) 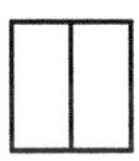
(D) 

2. What is the position of bead R from the top?

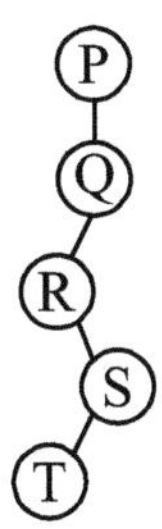

(A) First
(B) Third
(C) Fifth
(D) Fourth

3. Identify the shape or pattern that belongs to the group of the shapes given?

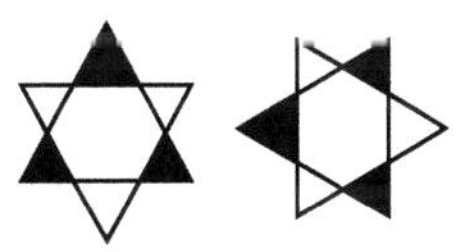

(A) 
(B) 
(C) 
(D) 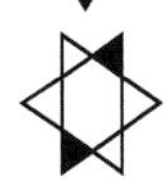

4. Count the number of standing lines in the given figure.

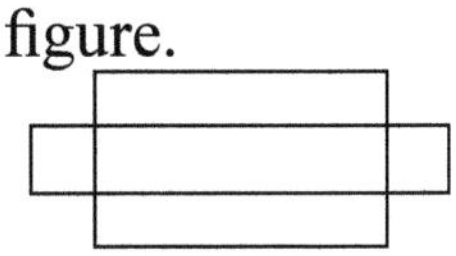

(A) 2
(B) 6
(C) 8
(D) 4

5. Choose the figure from the options in which figure (X) is exactly embedded as one of its part.

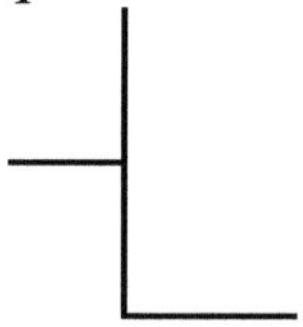

Fig. (X)

(A) 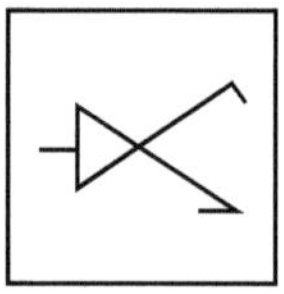 (B) 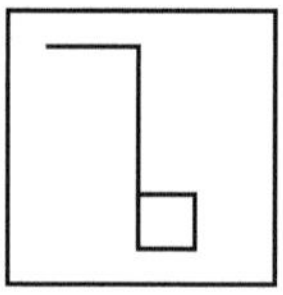

(C) 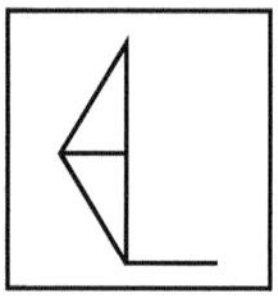 (D) 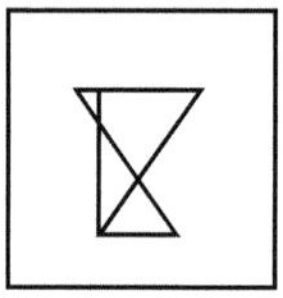

6. Which of the following objects is shortest?

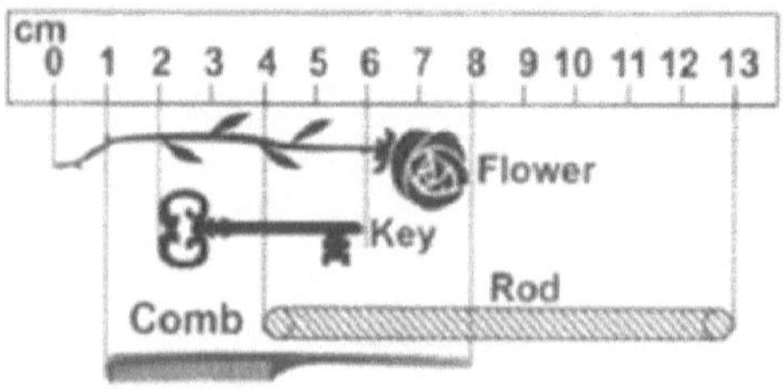

(A) Comb (B) Rod
(C) Flower (D) Key

7. If Monkey is called Fish, Fish is called Parrot and Parrot is called Dog, then which of the following lives in water?

(A) Parrot (B) Dog
(C) Fish (D) Monkey

8. Complete the second pair in the same way as the first pair.

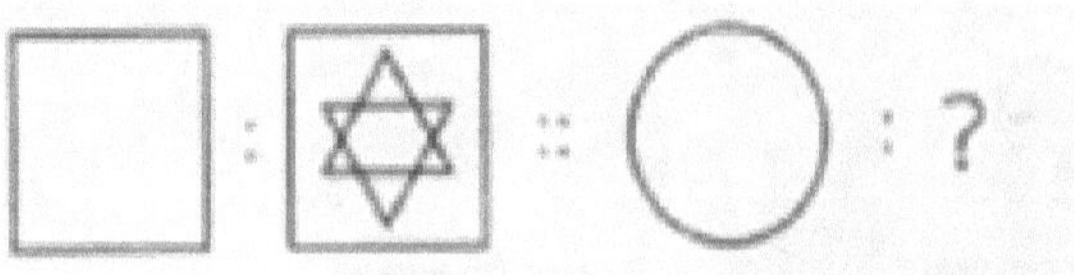

(A)  (B) 

(C)  (D) 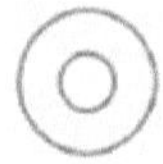

9. How many triangles and circles are there in the given figure?

(A) 2, 4 (B) 4, 2
(C) 3, 5 (D) 4, 1

10. Complete the series.

(A)  (B) 

(C)  (D) 

11. The picture graph shows the number of hot dogs sold during weekdays.

Day	Number of hot dogs sold
Monday	
Tuesday	
Wednesday	
Thursday	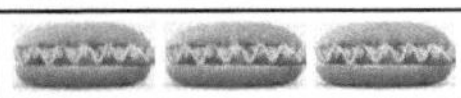
Each  stands for 10 hot dogs	

How many hot dogs were sold on Wednesday?

(A) 30 (B) 20

(C) 40 (D) 50

12. Harshita and Tanya had ₹ 300 in all. After spending ₹ 160, how much money did they save altogether?

(A) ₹ 460 (B) ₹ 140

(C) ₹ 240 (D) ₹ 40

13. Which of the following clocks shows half past 9?

(A) 

(B) 

(C) 

(D) 

14. Identify the largest three-digit number, which is odd?

(A) 100 (B) 999

(C) 111 (D) 333

15. Forty six rupees and twenty paise is the cost of one article sold in a shop. Which article are we talking about?

(A) 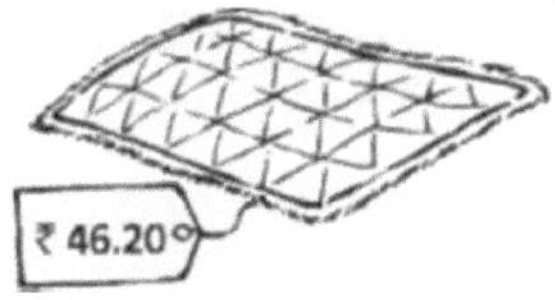

(B) 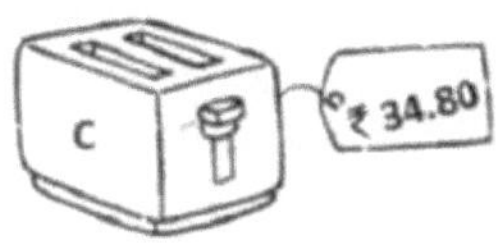

(C) 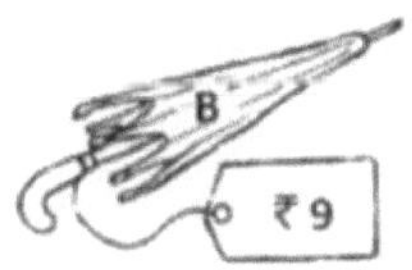

(D) 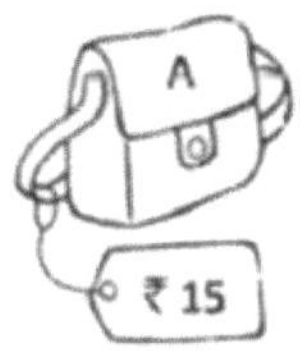

16. Arrange the following in descending order.

(A) 999, 945, 926, 932

(B) 999, 945, 932, 926

(C) 945, 999, 932, 926

(D) 932, 945, 926, 999

17. Which two pieces can be put together to form a square?

(A) 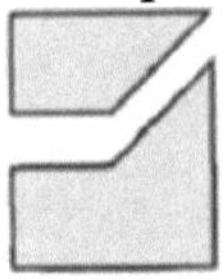 (B) 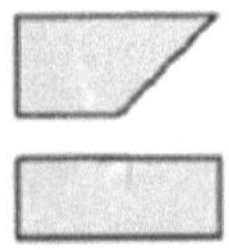

(C) 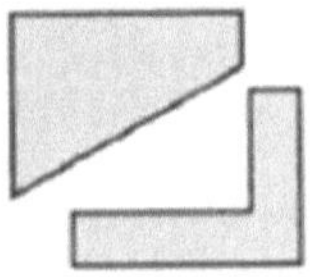 (D) 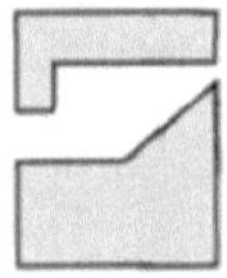

18. Which of the following has the least value?

(A) 32 ÷ 2 (B) 45 ÷ 3

(C) 50 ÷ 5 (D) 56 ÷ 4

19. By how much is 4 × 6 more than 3 + 3 + 3?

(A) 18 (B) 15

(C) 12 (D) 10

20. Which of the following numbers is same as 8 more than 30?

(A) 22 (B) 42

(C) 38 (D) 28

EVERYDAY MATHEMATICS

21. Shilpa had ₹ 180. Her brother gave her ₹ 20 for chips and her father gave her ₹ 100 for stationery. How much money she has now?

(A) ₹ 40 (B) ₹ 160

(C) ₹ 300 (D) ₹ 190

22. Megha is making a pattern. Which of the following objects will she use to trace the pattern of square?

(A)  (B) 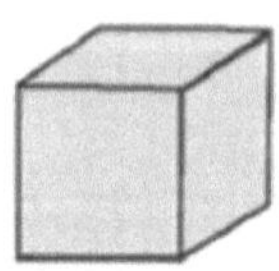

(C) 

(D) 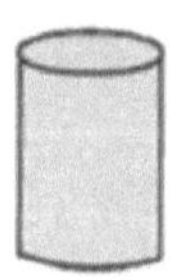

23. Manav bought 10 bags of wheat flour which weighs 120 kg. How much each bag weighs?

(A) 10 kg (B) 12 kg

(C) 8 kg (D) 1200 kg

24. Two students Akshay and Agam wrote a three-digit number on their boards respectively as shown.

Who wrote the greatest number?

(A) Agam

(B) Akshay

(C) Both (A) and (B)

(D) None of these

25. Sonam read a story book which has 162 pages. She has read 36 pages. How many pages are left?

(A) 116 (B) 126

(C) 136 (D) 139

26. The temperature in Jammu is 4 less than the temperature in Delhi. If the temperature in Delhi is 13°C, what will be temperature in Jammu?

(A) 17°C (B) 9°C
(C) 11°C (D) 15°C

27. A cat was sitting on 10. It jumped 5 times to reach 5. Which of the following represents correct option?

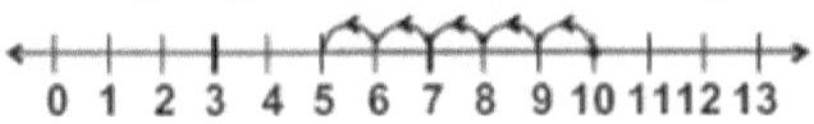

(A) 10 – 5 = 5
(B) 5 + 0 = 5
(C) 10 ÷ 5 = 2
(D) 10 + 5 = 15

28. Which option matches with the number name written on the given pencil?

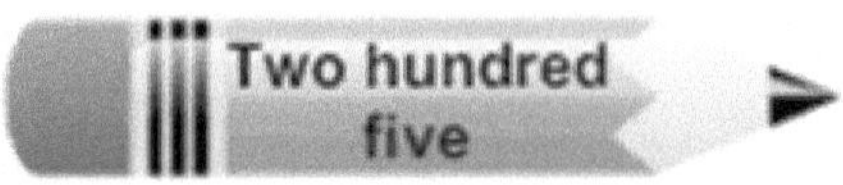

(A) 204 (B) 200
(C) 205 (D) 250

29. Ananya shares her birthday with Mahatma Gandhi. 15 days after her birthday is Monika's birthday. When will Monika's birthday be celebrated?
(A) 14 October
(B) 17 October
(C) 28 October
(D) 20 October

30. Mahi went to a stationery shop to buy a box of coloured pens having 12 pens. If each pen costs ₹ 10, how much does a box cost?

(A) ₹ 12 (B) ₹ 120
(C) ₹ 200 (D) ₹ 1200

ACHIEVERS SECTION

31. The annual meeting started at the given time in clock. The meeting was 2 hours and 20 minutes long. What time did the meeting end?

(A) 4 :15 (B) 12 : 15
(C) 2 : 08 (D) 1 : 15

32. Study the figure and answer the given question.

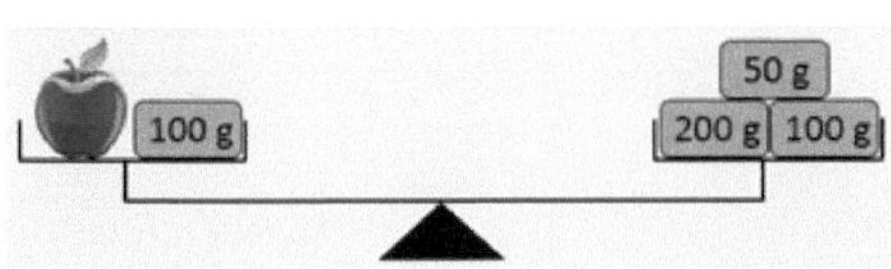

What is the weight of an apple?
(A) 250 g (B) 100 g
(C) 250 g (D) 300 g

33. Adarsh bought three different packs of chocolates. The cost of three packs are ₹ 50, ₹ 70, ₹ 45 respectively. Find the total amount he spent?
(A) ₹ 165 (B) ₹ 180
(C) ₹ 200 (D) ₹ 150

34. Mukul bought 7 boxes of pencils. Each box contains 12 pencils. He gave 20 pencils to his sister. How many pencils are left with him?
(A) 64 (B) 54
(C) 82 (D) 42

35. Study the figure and answer the given question.

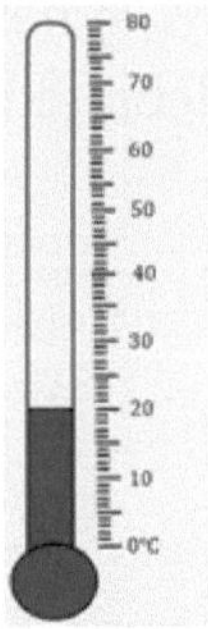

If room temperature is 5° less than the temperature shown on the given thermometer. Find the room temperature.

(A) 15° C (B) 10° C

(C) 25° C (D) 35° C

NATIONAL SCIENCE OLYMPIAD (NSO)

Mock Test Paper 1

N S O

NATIONAL SCIENCE OLYMPIAD

Total Questions : 35 Time : 1 Hour

PATTERN AND MARKING SCHEME			
Section	**(1) Logical Reasoning**	**(2) Science**	**(3) Achievers Section**
No. of Questions	5	25	5
Marks per Questions	1	1	2

SYLLABUS

Section – 1: Patterns, Measuring Units, Odd One Out, Series Completion, Geometrical Shapes, Analogy, Ranking Test, Grouping of Figures, Coding-Decoding, Embedded Figures.

Section – 2: Plants, Animals, Human Body, Food, Housing and Clothing, Family and Festivals, Occupations, Good Habits and Safety Rules, Transport and Communication, Air, Water and Rocks, Earth and Universe.

Section – 3: Higher Order Thinking Questions – Syllabus as per Section – 2.

LOGICAL REASONING

1. The clock is showing the time:

(A) Half an hour later to 2: 10
(B) Quarter to 3:00 O'clock
(C) Both of these
(D) None of these

2. Find out the best fitted part to complete the pattern.

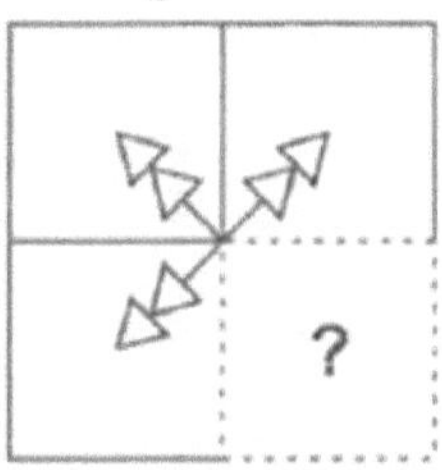

(A)  (B) 

(C)  (D) 

3. Horse : Hoof :: Cat : ?
(A) Foot (B) Paw
(C) Hoof (D) Palm

4. Megha is 12th from bottom and 16th from the top in the merit of the class. How many students are in the class?
(A) 27 (B) 28
(C) 29 (D) 30

5. In the given set of numbers find two odds.

3, 7, 9, 11, 13, 15

(A) 7, 9 (B) 11, 13
(C) 3, 15 (D) 9, 15

SCIENCE

6. The juice obtained from the crop in the given image is used to make _________.

(A) Sugar (B) Gum
(C) Rubber (D) Oil

7. The given images are obtained from which part of plant?

(A) Roots (B) Stems
(C) Leaves (D) None of these

8. Watermelon and bottle gourds are examples of which type of plant?
(A) Climbers
(B) Creepers
(C) Underground part
(D) None of these

9. Identify the set of domestic animals.
(A) Lion, elephant, buffalo
(B) Goat, dog, cow
(C) Beer, deer, cat
(D) All of these

10. Leather is made up of _________.
(A) Flesh part of cock
(B) Wings of peacock
(C) Skin of dead animals
(D) None of these

11. Our parents tell us to drink a glass of milk, the sensory organ they use is _________.
(A) Eyes (B) Tongue
(C) Nose (D) Ear

12. Refer to the given image and complete the sentence.

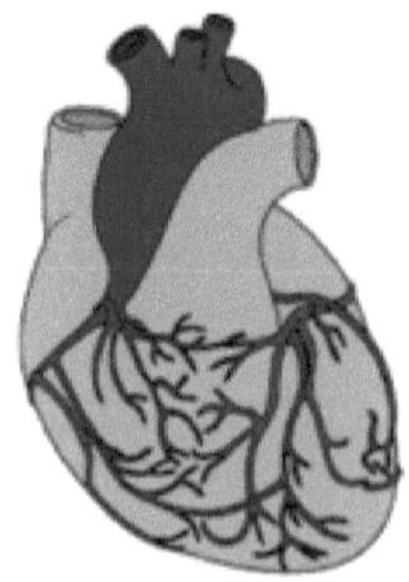

This is the image of our_______ and it _____ inside our body.
(A) Lungs, pumps the blood.
(B) Heart, transfer the oxygen.
(C) Lungs, transfer the oxygen.
(D) Heart, pumps the blood

13. Find the odd one out.

(A)  (B) 

(C)  (D) 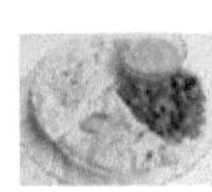

14. In the _____ method, food is preserved with the help of oil and excess salt.
    (A) Pickling (B) Jellying
    (C) Frying (D) Freezing
15. We get wool from_____ while____ give us cotton.
    (A) Plants, grass
    (B) Animals, grass
    (C) Animals, plants
    (D) Trees, plants
16. Observe the given picture carefully and identify the correct option.

    (A) This big house is made up of cement, bricks and other building material.
    (B) A single building contains many houses.
    (C) Each housc is called flat individually.
    (D) All of these.
17. Look at the image and fill in the blanks.

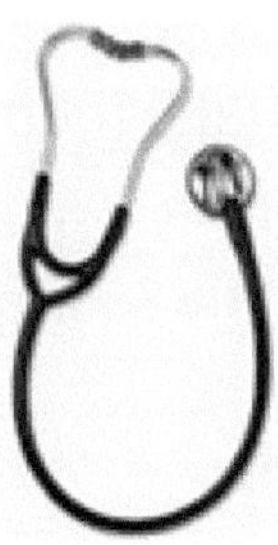

This is a ____ and a ____ uses it to check our heartbeat.
    (A) Earphones, engineer
    (B) Stethoscope, doctor
    (C) Stethoscope, engineer
    (D) None of these
18. This is the image of sewing tools. Who uses the sewing kits and tools to sew our clothes?

    (A) A tailor
    (B) A carpenter
    (C) A cobbler
    (D) An engineer
19. What activity should you not do when you are walking on the road?
    (A) Spitting on the road.
    (B) Crossing the road other than zebra crossing
    (C) Running in the middle of the road.
    (D) All of these

20. We should obey traffic rules in the same way as we follow traffic signal lights. Fill in the blanks about the signal lights.

Red light signals us to_____. Yellow light means we should ______ and green light signals to ________.

(A) Wait, stop, move
(B) Go, wait, move
(C) Stop, Wait, Go
(D) Wait, go, stop.

21. In the morning when you stand facing the sun, you are facing towards ____, on your right hand is____ on your back side it is _____ and on your left is ______.

(A) East, west, south, north
(B) East, south, west, north
(C) South, west, north, east
(D) East, north, west, south.

22. This is the image of ____.

(A) Bullock cart
(B) Wheel cart
(C) Horse cart
(D) None of these

23. What is the full form of PIN?

(A) Please inform number
(B) Permanent information number
(C) Permanent Index Number
(D) Postal Index Number

24. Identify the correct statement.

(A) Diamond is the hardest mineral.
(B) Gold and platinum are precious metals.
(C) Precious minerals are used for making of jewellery.
(D) All of these

25. What do we use to get groundwater?

(A) Wells
(B) Hand pumps
(C) Tube well
(D) All of these

26. The movement of the earth is known as _________.

(A) Rotation and revolution
(B) Rotation and reservation
(C) Revolution and evolution
(D) None of these

27. The atmosphere of the moon does not have____.

(A) Light
(B) Air
(C) Both of these
(D) None of these

28. Which of the following is our planet?

(A) Jupiter
(B) Mercury
(C) Venus
(D) Earth

29. Find the odd one out.

(A) 

(B) 

(C) 

(D) 

30. Biting your nails can make you____.
(A) Look bad
(B) Ill
(C) Both of these
(D) None of these

ACHIEVERS SECTION

31. We should not try to play with these things because they are harmful and dangerous for us. Why?

(A) Some of them are fire catcher, so they can burn us.
(B) Some of them have sharp edges so they can give us cuts and injuries.
(C) Some of them are very harmful chemicals, accidental engulf of those chemicals can harm our health badly.
(D) All of these

32. Prisha was travelling in the car with her parents. At a point she noticed three sign boards. She asked her father about the meaning of these sign boards. Her father explained her the meaning of the boards. What are the correct meanings of the given boards according to you?

(A) There is a hospital at left after some distance.
(B) Speed limit for small vehicles is 60 Km/hr and for large vehicles is 30 Km/hr
(C) They should not take a right turn.
(D) A, B and C are correct

33. If you observe the moon daily, you will see different shapes of moon everyday. Why does the shape of moon change everyday?

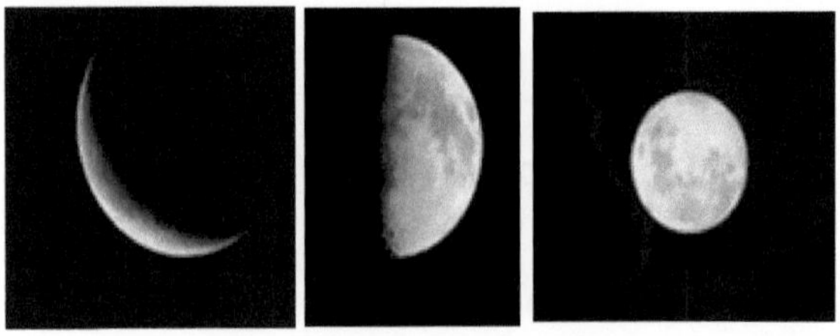

(A) The moon comes closer to the earth and then goes far from earth.
(B) The size of moon seems to grow first and then decrease. After full moon day the size of moon starts decreasing.
(C) Sun gives limited light to the moon.
(D) None of these

34. Observe the given image and mark the correct statements related to the image.

(A) It is the image of an ATM machine, it is used for withdrawing the money.
(B) We should stand in the queue and wait for our turn to withdraw money.
(C) We should not try to read the password of the person who is operating this machine.
(D) All of these

35. Observe the given chart and identify the correct option which are the suitable examples for d, e, f, g.

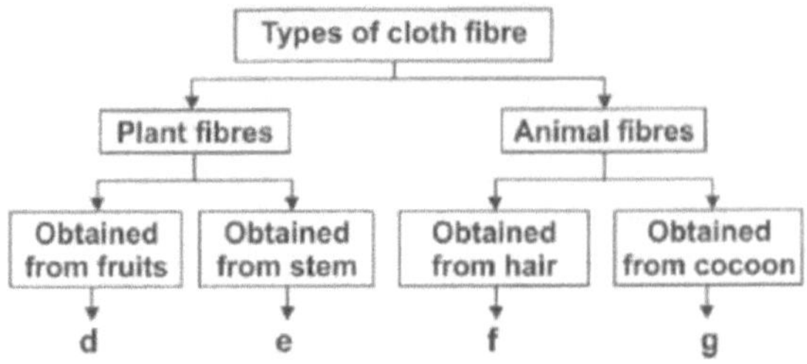

(A) Cotton, Jute, Wool, Silk
(B) Wool, Silk, Cotton, Jute
(C) Jute, Cotton, Wool, Silk
(D) Cotton, Jute, Silk, Wool

Mock Test Paper 2

N S O
NATIONAL SCIENCE OLYMPIAD

Total Questions : 35 Time : 1 Hour

PATTERN AND MARKING SCHEME			
Section	**(1) Logical Reasoning**	**(2) Science**	**(3) Achievers Section**
No. of Questions	5	25	5
Marks per Questions	1	1	2

SYLLABUS

Section – 1: Patterns, Measuring Units, Odd One Out, Series Completion, Geometrical Shapes, Analogy, Ranking Test, Grouping of Figures, Coding-Decoding, Embedded Figures.

Section – 2: Plants, Animals, Human Body, Food, Housing and Clothing, Family and Festivals, Occupations, Good Habits and Safety Rules, Transport and Communication, Air, Water and Rocks, Earth and Universe.

Section – 3: Higher Order Thinking Questions – Syllabus as per Section – 2.

LOGICAL REASONING

1. We love eating the pizza. A full pizza looks like a ____ and when we cut out a piece of the pizza, the shape of that piece is _____.
   (A) Circle, triangle
   (B) Ball, square
   (C) Circle, square
   (D) Cube, cube

2. Divide different shapes in different groups.

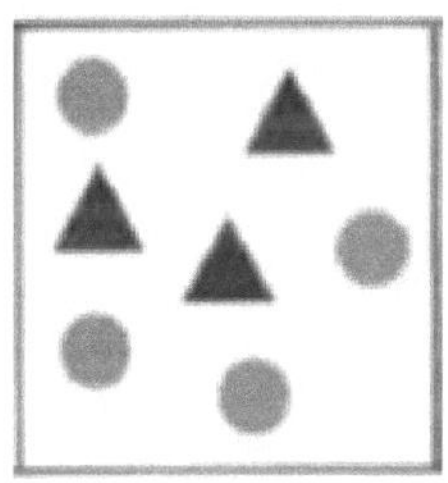

   (A) 2 triangles, 4 circles
   (B) 4 circles, 3 triangles
   (C) Any of these
   (D) None of these

3. If BAD can be written as 214, then SAD can be written as __________.
   (A) 1914 (B) 214
   (C) 4119 (D) None of these

4. Mark the figure from the options which in which the given image is completely embedded.

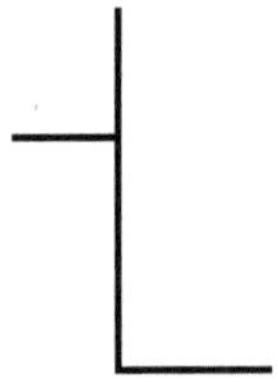

(A)  (B) 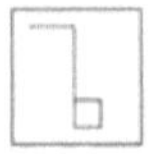

(C)  (D) 

5. What comes at the place of question mark in the following series 3, 6, 12, 24, ?

(A) 12 (B) 30

(C) 48 (D) 42

SCIENCE

6. Bicycle is an example of__________.

(A) Slow land transport

(B) Fast land transport

(C) Both of these

(D) None of these

7. Submarine belongs to which type of transportation?

(A) Air transport

(B) Underwater transport

(C) Land transport

(D) None of these

8. Which of the following is the natural satellite of our planet?

(A) Mercury (B) Moon

(C) Jupitar (D) Sun

9. Observe the image and guess the time?

(A) It's sunrise

(B) It's moonrise

(C) It's sunset

(D) It's moonset

10. What is the sun?

(A) A huge fire ball

(B) A huge star

(C) Both of these

(D) None of these

11. What are the parts of solar system?

(A) Moon and earth

(B) Sun and 8 planets

(C) Sun and earth

(D) Moon and stars

12. Mark the hardest mineral.

(A) Talc

(B) Quartz

(C) Diamond
(D) Graphite

13. You should reuse the water you once used. For example, the water you used for cleaning the vegetable, you should use it to flush the toilets. This reusing and recycling practise is called as __________.
(A) Water conservation
(B) Water pollution
(C) Water harvesting
(D) All of these

14. The person who can not speak and cannot hear, can communicate through which language?
(A) Foreign language
(B) Sign language
(C) Eye language
(D) None of these

15. Your grandparents live in another city. You want to see them, and your mother helps you to see them through electronic telecommunication. You are seeing them through_____.
(A) Video calling
(B) E-mail
(C) Voice calling
(D) None of these

16. Mark the outdoor game.
(A)  (B) 
(C)  (D) 

17. Suppose, you are playing in a big ground. Suddenly, your best friend gets hurt and starts bleeding. What should you do?
(A) Continue playing.
(B) Rub some sand on his wounds.
(C) Call elder people for help and give him first aid
(D) Start crying because your friend is crying.

18. Who is the person given in the image?

(A) An army man
(B) A doctor
(C) A policeman
(D) A fireman

19. What does a potter do?
(A) He makes shoes
(B) He repairs the shows
(C) He makes the pots
(D) All of these

20. In the chilly cold winters Pritha is standing in a room and staring at the bucket full of water. She screamed "Oh God! It is so cold, I don't want to touch cold water".
Now name the room where Pritha is present at this time.
(A) Study room (B) Bathroom
(C) Bedroom (D) None of these

21. Refer the image and complete the following sentence.

It is a type of house and is known as _____. These houses are also called ______. These houses are built by _____.

(A) Igloo, snow hut, eskimo

(B) White house, snow house, hill man

(C) Igloo, white house, snow man

(D) White house, snow house, eskimo

22. In one day, we should take heaviest meal as our _____, and lightest meal as our_____.

(A) Lunch, dinner

(B) Breakfast, dinner

(C) Breakfast, lunch

(D) None of these

23. Fish, nuts, milk, eggs can be put into the _______ food group.

(A) Protective food

(B) Energy giving food

(C) Body building food

(D) All of these

24. Mark the correct statement about the shape of human body.

(A) It is made up of bones and muscles.

(B) Muscles help in the movement of bones.

(C) Bones give support and shape to the body.

(D) All of these

25. Our body frame is made up of bones, the framework is called as ________.

(A) Skeleton

(B) Backbone

(C) Brain

(D) None of these

26. Cow: Calf :: Kangaroo: ?

(A) Puppy (B) Kitten

(C) Joeys (D) Mule

27. We should not harm animals. What activity should we not do with animals?

(A) Harm them by binding firecrackers in the tails of animals.

(B) Harm them by throwing stones on them.

(C) Hunting them to eat.

(D) All of them

28. Identify the correct difference between young plant and adult plant.

(A) Young plants have roots while adult plants do not have roots.

(B) Young plants do not have flowers while adult plants have flowers.

(C) Young plants do not grow while adult plants grow.

(D) Young plant does not have a stem while adult plants have stem.

29. If we remove all the leaves from the plants, what will be the result of this action?
(A) They will not be able to make their food.
(B) They will fall on the ground.
(C) They will stop transferring water in all the parts.
(D) They will stop taking nutrients from the soil.

30. This is the image of pine trees. What do we obtain from pine trees?

(A) Fruits (B) Flowers
(C) Wood (D) Vegetables

ACHIEVERS SECTION

31. What are the similarities between these two plants?

(A) Their stems are weak
(B) Their stems are woody
(C) Both flowers produce seeds
(D) B and C are correct

32. The given objects are obtained from some animals. Identify the correct match.

(A) 1- Sheep, 2- crocodile
(B) 2- Yak, 3- Sheep
(C) 2- Yak, 3- crocodile
(D) 1- Silk worm, 2- crocodile

33. Suppose, in a school activity you have been blindfolded. What differences can you observe even when you cannot see the objects?
(A) Two different papers with different colors
(B) Two different flowers
(C) Two different juices
(D) B and C

34. What could be P, Q and R

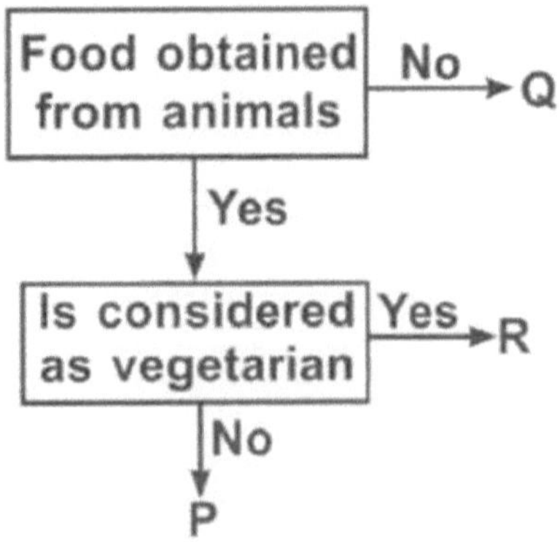

(A) P is obtained from cow, Q is obtained from Chicken
(B) P and Q both are given by cow
(C) R is given by cow, P is given by chicken
(D) None of these

35. The process of making clothes from wool yarn is called as ___________.
(A) Waving (B) Sewing
(C) Weaving (D) None of these

NATIONAL CYBER OLYMPIAD (NCO)

Mock Test Paper 1

N C O

NATIONAL CYBER OLYMPIAD

Total Questions : 35 Time : 1 Hour

PATTERN AND MARKING SCHEME			
Section	**(1) Logical Reasoning**	**(2) Computer and IT**	**(3) Achievers Section**
No. of Questions	5	25	5
Marks per Questions	1	1	2

SYLLABUS

Section – 1: Patterns, Measuring Units, Odd One Out, Series Completion, Geometrical Shapes, Analogy, Ranking Test, Grouping of Figures, Coding-Decoding, Embedded Figures.

Section – 2: Computer-a Smart Machine, General Information about Computers, Parts of Computer, Uses of Computer, Learning to use Keyboard and Mouse, MS Paint, Latest Developments in the field of IT.

Section – 3: Higher Order Thinking Questions – Syllabus as per Section – 2.

LOGICAL REASONING

1. Choose the figure which will complete the following pattern.

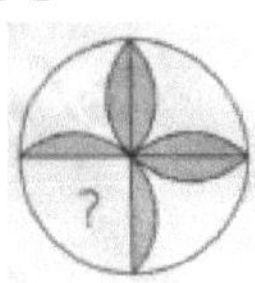

(A) 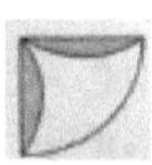 (B) 

(C)  (D) 

2. How many groups of 3 butterflies can be formed?

(A) 6 (B) 5
(C) 2 (D) 7

3. Find the missing figure.

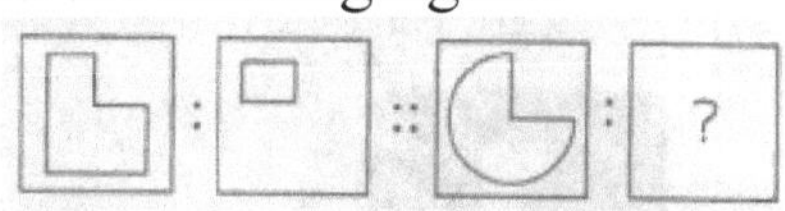

(A) 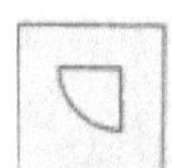 (B) 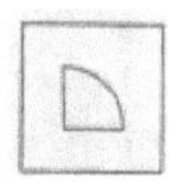

(C)  (D) 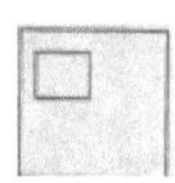

4. If mirror is called phone, phone is called television and television is called window, then which of the following is used for calling?

(A) Mirror (B) Window
(C) Television (D) None of these

5. Identify the figure in which the given figure (X) is hidden.

(X)

(A) 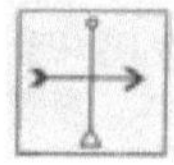 (B) 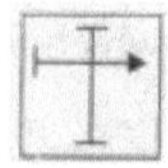

(C)  (D) 

COMPUTERS AND IT

6. Which of the following is an output device?

(A)  (B) 

(C)  (D) 

7. _____________ is a special space used to store files. It is also known as directory.
(A) Folder (B) Icon
(C) Files (D) None of these

8. Name the following.
The sequence of actions done by the computer to get everything ready for use, while starting.
(A) Logging (B) Clicking
(C) Booting (D) None of these

9. Which of the following options will help you to shut down the computer safely and then starts it again?
(A) Shut Down (B) Sleep
(C) Log off (D) Restart

10. Identify the following.
It a major component of the central processing unit of a computer system.
It is used to perform arithmetic and logic operations.
(A) VDU (B) ALU
(C) CPU (D) None of these

11. ____________ is the name assigned to a user to access a computer.
(A) Username (B) Password
(C) Tools (D) Icons

12. A _______ is a wire through which several devices can be connected to the computer.
(A) Webcam (B) Mouse
(C) Data cable (D) None of these

13. Select the correct match.

(A)  – Joystick

(B)  – Microphone

(C)  – CPU

(D)  – Speakers

14. Identify the device by the statement given below.

    An input device that captures a video image of the scene in front of it.

    It is also used for video chat sessions with other people.

    (A) Printer (B) Web camera
    (C) Scanner (D) Microphone

15. The secret combination of alphabets and numbers to have access to the computer is called __________

    (A) Wallpaper (B) Password
    (C) Username (D) None of these

16. Page Up, Page Down, Home, End are the ________ keys.

    (A) Navigation keys
    (B) Function keys
    (C) Special keys
    (D) Alphabet keys

17. What is the utility of the action of mouse being displayed in the figure given below?

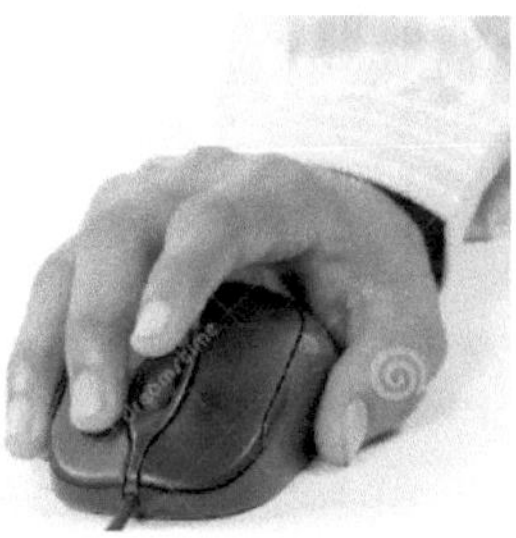

    (A) It is used for selecting an item on screen.
    (B) It is used for opening a document.
    (C) It displays list of commands on the screen.
    (D) None of these

18. Identify X.

    It is used to switch between numbers and symbols, and capital and small letters.

    It is used in combination with a letter key when the Caps Lock key is OFF.

    (A) Spacebar key
    (B) Shift key
    (C) Delete key
    (D) Backspace key

19. Which of the following key opens the Start menu?

    (A) 

    (B) 

    (C) 

    (D) 

20. Select the correct match.

    (A) Banks- Booking Tickets
    (B) Entertainment – Designing and printing books.
    (C) Shopping Malls- Billing
    (D) Publishing- Withdrawal of money through ATM.

21. Where does a computer process the information?

    (A) 
    (B) 
    (C) 
    (D) 

22. Identify the type of mouse.

(A) Ball Mouse
(B) Optical Mouse
(C) Tactile Mouse
(D) None of these

23. Identify the icon.

(A) Paste (B) Copy
(C) Cut (D) Paint

24. Which of the following shows the correct sequence of IPO cycle?

(A) 

(B) 

(C) 

(D) All of these

25. What does app stand for?
(A) Application (B) Applicant
(C) Apply (D) None of these

26. Identify the logo of Xiaomi phone.

(A) (B)

(C) (D)

27. Select odd one out in context with tools found in MS Paint program.

(A)  (B) 

(C)  (D) 

28. Which of the following is a social networking site?

(A) (B)

(C) (D) All of these

29. Unscramble the word given below and select the device on which it is found.

LOSCRL LHEEW

(A) Mouse (B) Printer
(C) Microphone (D) Web Camera

30. UPS stands for _________.
(A) Uninterruptible Power System
(B) Uninterrupted Power Supply
(C) Unlimited Power Supply
(D) None of these

31. Which of the following keys move the cursor up, down, left or right without erasing characters?
   (A) Toggle key
   (B) Escape key
   (C) Navigation keys
   (D) Arrow keys

32. Identify the action of mouse with the help of given information.
   It is used to move an item on the screen by keeping the left mouse button pressed without releasing it, then releasing the button where you want to place the item.
   (A) Single click
   (B) Double click
   (C) Drag and drop
   (D) None of these

33. Which of the following statement is true for the given device?

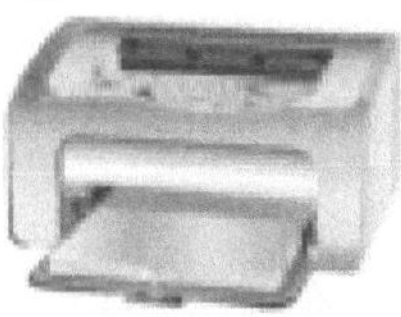

   (A) It looks like a TV screen.
   (B) It shows the hard copy of the output.
   (C) It keeps the computer working in case of power failure.
   (D) None of these

34. The given screen appears when you click on ________ button.

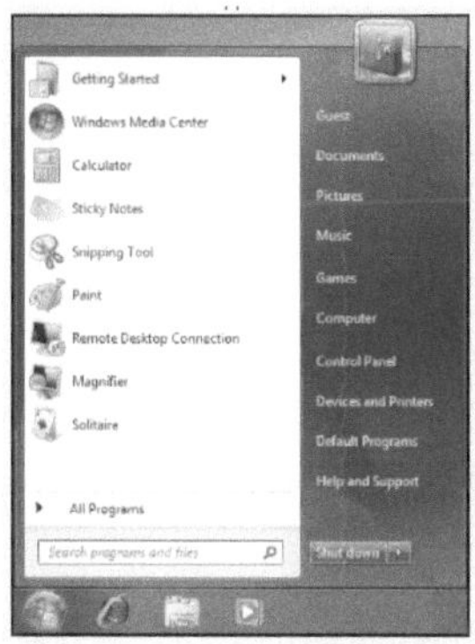

   (A) Recycle bin (B) Shut down
   (C) Start (D) None of these

35. Match the following.

Column I		Column II	
A.		(i)	Shut Down
B.	Turning Off the computer	(ii)	UPS
C.	Processing unit	(iii)	Text tool
D.	Device used during power failure	(iv)	CPU

   (A) A-(iii), B-(i), C-(iv), D-(ii)
   (B) A-(i), B-(iv), C-(iii), D-(ii)
   (C) A-(ii), B-(i), C-(iii), D-(iv)
   (D) A-(iv), B-(i), C-(ii), D-(iii)

Mock Test Paper 2

N C O
NATIONAL CYBER OLYMPIAD

Total Questions : 35 Time : 1 Hour

PATTERN AND MARKING SCHEME			
Section	**(1) Logical Reasoning**	**(2) Computer and IT**	**(3) Achievers Section**
No. of Questions	5	25	5
Marks per Questions	1	1	2

SYLLABUS

Section – 1: Patterns, Measuring Units, Odd One Out, Series Completion, Geometrical Shapes, Analogy, Ranking Test, Grouping of Figures, Coding-Decoding, Embedded Figures.

Section – 2: Computer-a Smart Machine, General Information about Computers, Parts of Computer, Uses of Computer, Learning to use Keyboard and Mouse, MS Paint, Latest Developments in the field of IT.

Section – 3: Higher Order Thinking Questions – Syllabus as per Section – 2.

LOGICAL REASONING

1. Complete the second pair by choosing a figure from given alternatives.

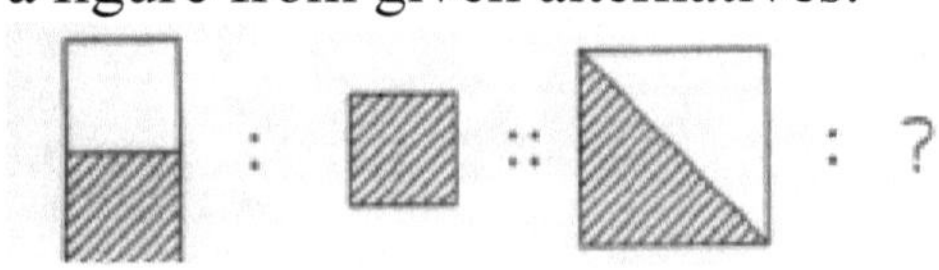

(A)  (B) 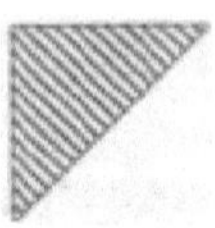

(C)  (D) 

2. Complete the following series.

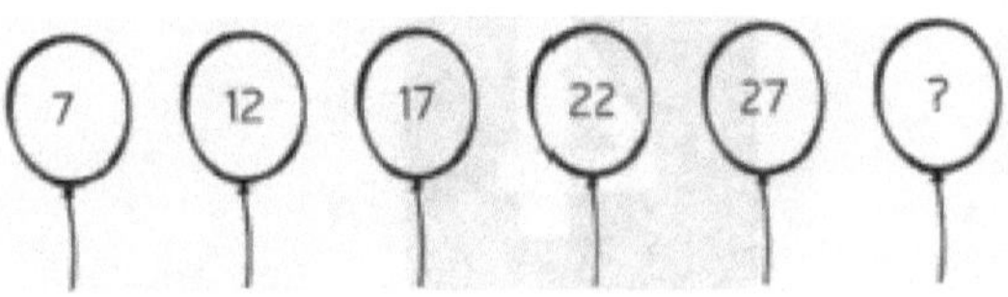

(A) 32 (B) 37
(C) 44 (D) 58

3. Priya ranked 11th from the top and 27th from the bottom in a class. How many students are there in the class?
(A) 39 (B) 38
(C) 45 (D) 37

4. Select the figure in which the given figure (X) is embedded as one of its part.

(X)

(A)  (B) 

(C) 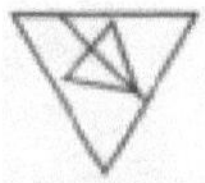 (D) 

5. If the code for DARE is ERAD, then what will be the code for 7826?
(A) 6287 (B) 8726
(C) 7682 (D) 2687

COMPUTERS AND IT

6. Which of the following parts provide power supply to our computer during power failure?
(A)  (B) 
(C)  (D) 

7. ______ is the unit of speed of a computer.
(A) Hertz (B) Decibel
(C) MHz (D) Bytes

8. Which of the following tasks can be done with the help of device shown here?

(A) To play games on the computer
(B) To type letters on screen
(C) To point icons on screen
(D) To capture a video image of the scene in front of it.

9. Which of the following types of computers are considered to be large computers and can do huge calculations?
(A) Laptop
(B) Supercomputers
(C) Palmtop
(D) None of these

10. The bar that appears at the bottom of the desktop is __________.
(A) Taskbar
(B) Menu Bar
(C) Window Bar
(D) None of these

11. Name the device that enables you to record your voice, music and sounds.
(A) Joystick (B) Speakers
(C) Microphone (D) Scanner

12. Which of the following keys is used to move cursor several spaces forward at once?
(A) Tab key
(B) Shift key
(C) Delete key
(D) Spacebar key

13. ______ click displays list of commands on the screen.
(A) Double (B) Right
(C) Single (D) None of these

14. Identify the following.

It helps us to play games on computer.

It has a long lever and buttons on it to play games.

(A) Microphone (B) Web Camera
(C) Joystick (D) Printer

15. __________ is the place where you can draw and colour pictures.

(A) Paint screen window
(B) Drawing Area
(C) Ribbon Area
(D) None of these

16. Which of the following action of mouse is used to open a document?

(A) Double clicking
(B) Single clicking
(C) Scrolling
(D) None of these

17. Identify the key by the statements given below.

It is the longest key on the keyboard.

It is used to give space after words, alphabets or numbers. If pressed once, it gives the space of one character.

(A) Delete key
(B) Shift Key
(C) Backspace key
(D) Spacebar key

18. Which of the following tasks cannot be done on smartwatch?

(A) Playing games
(B) Solving sums
(C) listening to music
(D) Writing story

19. Name the key that is used in combination with other keys for special functions.

(A) Tab key
(B) Ctrl and Alt key
(C) Enter key
(D) Esc key

20. In the word given below, cursor has been placed after the letter A.

Rela|te

Which of the following keys when pressed will remove the letter A before the cursor?

(A) Backspace key
(B) Delete key
(C) Shift key
(D) Enter key

21. Which of the following statements is/are incorrect about the given device?

(A) It is designed to be used by a one person at a time.
(B) It can be carried from one place to another.
(C) It works on a battery and can easily fit in your lap.
(D) It is bigger than the desktop.

22. __________ is the latest version of iPhone.

(A) iPhone 6 plus
(B) iPhone 4S
(C) iPhone XS
(D) None of these

23. Which of the following statements hold(s) true regarding single click?

Statement 1: Pressing the left mouse button once and then releasing it is called single click.

Statement 2: It is used for selecting an item on screen.

(A) Only Statement 2
(B) Both statement 1 and 2
(C) Only statement 1
(D) None of these

24. Sonia has to draw a picture of garden which is rectangular in shape. Which tool should she use to draw a picture?

(A) 

(B) 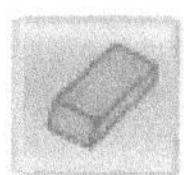
(C) 
(D) None of these

25. Identify the given icon.

(A) Copy (B) Cut
(C) Table (D) Pages

26. Which key combination will you use to insert the '%' symbol in a document?

(A) 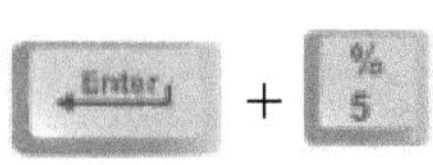

(B) 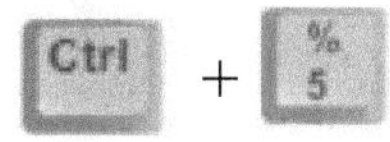

(C) 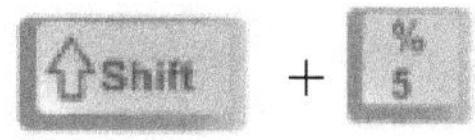

(D) 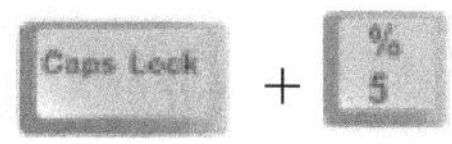

27. Select the correct match.

(A) Schools- keeping employee records
(B) Offices- Preparing medical reports
(C) Hospitals- Keeping records of books in the library.
(D) Banks- withdrawal of money through ATM

28. The ________ is used to move a page up and down by rolling it.

(A) Right button (B) Scroll wheel
(C) Left button (D) None of these

29. IPO stands for __________.

(A) Input process output
(B) Initial progress output
(C) Initial process output
(D) None of these

30. Which tool will help you to fill the entire picture with color in MS-paint?

(A) Pencil (B) Oval
(C) Color (D) Rectangle

ACHIEVERS SECTION

31. Select the incorrect match.

(A) To write any text - 

(B) To change the size for a part of a picture - 

(C) To delete the selected object - 

(D) Used to cut the selected part - 

32. Unscramble the jumbled word given below and select the correct statement about it.

STJIOCYK

(A) It is not a pointing device.

(B) It is used to record your voice, music and sounds in the computer.

(C) It is used to play games on the computer.

(D) None of these

33. Identify the following.

It is present twice on keyboard.

It is used to move the cursor to the next line.

(A) 

(B) 
(C) 
(D) 

34. Arrange the following steps in correct sequence to create a folder on desktop.

1. Click on "New".
2. Type the name of the folder and press Enter key.
3. Click on "Folder"
4. Right click on desktop.

(A) 2, 1, 3, 4 (B) 4, 1, 3, 2

(C) 1, 3, 4, 2 (D) 3, 2, 4, 1

35. Match the following

Column I		Column II	
A.	Key used to cancel any command action	(i)	Moves an item on screen
B.	Drag and drop	(ii)	Icons
C.	To activate numeric keypad on keyboard	(iii)	 Esc
D.	Small pictures on the desktop screen	(iv)	Num Lock

(A) A-(i), B-(iv), C-(iii), D-(ii)

(B) A-(iv), B-(i), C-(ii), D-(iii)

(C) A-(iii), B-(i), C-(iv), D-(ii)

(D) A-(ii), B-(i), C-(iii), D-(iv)

INTERNATIONAL ENGLISH OLYMPIAD (IEO)

Mock Test Paper 1

I E O

INTERNATIONAL ENGLISH OLYMPIAD

Total Questions : 35 Time : 1 Hour

PATTERN AND MARKING SCHEME				
Section	(1) Word and Structure Knowledge	(2) Reading	(3) Spoken and Written Expression	(4)Achievers
No. of Questions		30		5
Marks per Questions		1		2

SYLLABUS

Section – 1 : Collocations, Spellings, Synonyms, Antonyms, Identify the word from the Picture, Words Related to Animals, Nouns, Pronouns, Verbs, Adverbs, Adjectives, Articles, Prepositions, Conjunctions, Contractions, Word Order, Punctuation, Simple Tenses.

Section – 2 : Search for and retrieve information from various text types like Stories, Short Dialogues, etc. Acquire broad understanding of and look for specific information in short texts like Messages, Invitations, etc.

Section – 3 : Ability to understand situation-based variations in functions like Thanking, Greeting, Asking for Permission, Introducing (oneself), etc.

Section – 4 : Higher Order Thinking Questions - Syllabus as per Sections 1, 2 and 3.

WORD AND STRUCTURE KNOWLEDGE

1. Identify the common noun from the following.
   (A) newspaper
   (B) The Time Express
   (C) The Hindu
   (D) Dainik Jagran

2. Fill in the blank with the suitable pronoun.
   The sunlight does not reach the room properly, so __ is very dark.
   (A) That (B) This
   (C) It (D) They

3. Fill in the blanks with the appropriate adjectives related to the following image.

   This chocolate cake is ___ and ___.
   (A) Big, round
   (B) square, big
   (C) Small, beautiful
   (D) Layered, small

4. Identify the verb in the following sentence.

A mother cooks food for her children.

(A) Cook (B) Mother
(C) Her (D) For

5. Identify the adverb in the following sentence.

We should study everyday.

(A) Study (B) Should
(C) Everyday (D) Every

6. Fill in the blank with suitable preposition.

The chair is made __ wood.

(A) To (B) Of
(C) With (D) On

7. Identify the conjunction in the following sentence.

You can buy a black skirt or blank pant to wear it in the function.

(A) Can (B) Buy
(C) Or (D) to

8. Fill in the blanks with the suitable articles.

Her mother is __ engineer and her father is __ doctor.

(A) the, an (B) an, an
(C) a, an (D) an, a

9. Identify the pair of words which can be contracted to replace the words in the given sentence.

I have a younger brother. He is very intelligent.

(A) Have + a (B) He + is
(C) He + very (D) A + younger.

10. Complete the following sentence with suitable collocation.

Let's ___ our experience on a paper, about the trip.

(A) write up (B) mark up
(C) speak up (D) look up

11. Find the correct spelling.

(A) Across (B) Accros
(C) Accross (D) Acroos

12. Arrange the following shuffled words in a proper manner to make a sentence.

Like/ cricket/ father/ with/ I/ playing/ my

(A) My father like playing cricket with I
(B) Playing cricket I like with my father
(C) I like playing cricket with my father
(D) Father like playing my cricket with I

13. Identify the appropriate punctuations to replace the question marks in the following sentence.

Hurray _?_ I won the race_?_

(A) Exclamatory mark (!) and full stop (.)
(B) Question mark (?) and full stop (.)
(C) Full stop (.) and question mark (?)
(D) Full stop (.) and Exclamatory mark (!)

14. Mark the correct option which is the synonym of the underlined word in the following sentence.

Swami Vivekananda was a very <u>intelligent</u> man.

(A) Wise (B) Angry
(C) Cunning (D) Smart

15. Identify the correct antonym word to fill in the blank of the following sentence. The word should be antonym to the word given in the bracket.

Amit's handwriting is ___ than me. (better)

(A) Good (B) Best
(C) Worse (D) Worst

16. Which sport the kids are playing in the given picture?

(A) Baseball (B) Tennis
(C) Volleyball (D) Badminton

17. What kind of sound a chimpanzee makes?

(A) Meow (B) Bark
(C) Roar (D) Scream

18. Which of the following is/are a domestic animal(s)?

(A) Cow (B) Dog
(C) Horse (D) All of these

19. Which of the following is not a gregarious animal?

(A) Penguin (B) Wolf
(C) Polar bear (D) Duck

20. What is the helping verb of past indefinite tense?

(A) Does (B) Did
(C) Do (D) Will

21. Today we will not go to play because it __ raining heavily.

Fill in the blank with the suitable helping verb.

(A) Is (B) Am
(C) Are (D) Will

22. Identify the tense from the following sentence.

The gardener was giving water to the plants.

(A) Present continuous tense
(B) Past indefinite tense
(C) Past progressive/ continuous tense
(D) Present indefinite tense

23. Fill in the blank with the help of hint given in the bracket.

I ____ my tiffin with my best friend. (share)

(A) Share (B) Sharing
(C) Shared (D) Sharen

READING

24. Observe the image carefully and answer the question.

Anant and Shiksha are playing _____.

(A) Tic tac toe (B) Chess
(C) Ludo (D) Snake and ladder

Read the poem and answer the questions 25 and 26.

" The sky is dark, and the ground is white.
The world is peaceful on this wintry night.
No one around, not a sound to be heard.
Not a laugh, not a car, not even a bird.
For a moment it is just snow and me.
I smile inside. I am free."

25. What is the colour of sky in the wintry night?

(A) Dark (B) White
(C) Bright (D) Blue

26. Why the colour of the ground is white?

(A) Because of winters
(B) Because the sky is dark
(C) Because of snow on the ground
(D) Because the world is peaceful

SPOKEN AND WRITTEN EXPRESSIONS

27. Fill in the blanks with proper punctuation.

We generally hear an announcement on the platform _____(i) the train number 01234 is arriving on the platform number 1 shortly_____(ii)

	(i)	(ii)		(i)	(ii)
(A)	?	!	(B)	;	!
(C)	,	!	(D)	;	.

28. Identify the correctly punctuated sentence.

(A) It was a tiring day so she slept in the class
(B) It was, a tiring day so, she slept in the class!
(C) It was a tiring day, so she slept in the class.
(D) It was, a tiring day, so, she , slept in the class.

29. Diksha: __?__

Teacher: Yes, you may come in.

(A) May I go out of the class, teacher?
(B) May I come in, teacher?
(C) May I speak something, teacher?
(D) Will you allow me to come in, teacher?

30. Identify the sentence which supports the continuity of the sentence 1.

Mehjabeen was playing in the ground.

(A) Playing in the ground is not good.

(B) There were many children playing in the ground.

(C) She may fall ill.

(D) Ground is so dirty.

ACHIEVERS SECTION

31. The green ball bounced all over the small room.

Identify noun, adjective and verb.

	Noun	Adjective	Verb
(A)	Ball, Room	Green, small	Jumped
(C)	Green, small	Ball, room	Jumped
(D)	Small room	Green ball	All over

32. Provide a single word for the underlined group of words.

I offered my services to my neighbours, but they <u>did not accept it</u>.

(A) Refused (B) Accepted

(C) Avoided (D) Governed

33. Identify the alternative sentence placing feminine term in the place of masculine term in the following sentence.

The emperor of Maharashtra was so powerful that he won many battles against enemies.

(A) The empress of Maharashtra was so powerful that she won many battles against enemies.

(B) The female emperor of Maharashtra was so powerful that she won many battles against enemies.

(C) The male emperor of Maharashtra was so powerful that he won many battles against female.

(D) The empress of Maharashtra was so powerful that she won many battles against men.

34. Select the proper contraction which can be used in the following sentence.

Taj Mahal is a beautiful monument. It was built by Shahjahan. ___ situated in Agra.

(A) He's (B) She's

(C) It's (D) That's

35. Unscramble the conjunction to correctly complete the following sentence.

Meghna and Reshma are twin sisters ___ they look different from each other.

(A) nda (B) nac

(C) eht (D) tub

Mock Test Paper 2

Total Questions : 35 Time : 1 Hour

I E O
INTERNATIONAL ENGLISH OLYMPIAD

PATTERN AND MARKING SCHEME				
Section	(1) Word and Structure Knowledge	(2) Reading	(3) Spoken and Written Expression	(4)Achievers
No. of Questions		30		5
Marks per Questions		1		2

Syllabus

Section – 1 : Collocations, Spellings, Synonyms, Antonyms, Identify the word from the Picture, Words Related to Animals, Nouns, Pronouns, Verbs, Adverbs, Adjectives, Articles, Prepositions, Conjunctions, Contractions, Word Order, Punctuation, Simple Tenses.

Section – 2 : Search for and retrieve information from various text types like Stories, Short Dialogues, etc. Acquire broad understanding of and look for specific information in short texts like Messages, Invitations, etc.

Section – 3 : Ability to understand situation-based variations in functions like Thanking, Greeting, Asking for Permission, Introducing (oneself), etc.

Section – 4 : Higher Order Thinking Questions - Syllabus as per Sections 1, 2 and 3.

WORD AND STRUCTURE KNOWLEDGE

1. Read the following sentence carefully and identify the tense.
   She does not like coffee.
   (A) Present indefinite tense
   (B) Past indefinite tense
   (C) Future indefinite tense
   (D) I don't know.

2. Fill in the blank with the hint given in the bracket.
   The Sun __ in the East. (rise)
   (A) rises (B) rose
   (C) rosen (D) rised

3. Sachin Tendulkar __ a famous cricket player. (helping verb)
   (A) are (B) am
   (C) is (D) did

4. I __ go to school tomorrow. (helping verb)
   (A) Will (B) Shall
   (C) Does (D) Had

5. Identify the set of animals which are herbivores.
   (A) Elephant, Lion
   (B) Deer, Cat
   (C) Elephant, Horse
   (D) Horse, Dog

6. What is a baby of monkey called?

(A) Calf (B) Infant
(C) Colt (D) Filly

7. What is a group of dogs called?
(A) Herd (B) Dove
(C) Heap (D) Pack

8. Choose the right word for the picture.

(A) Dancing
(B) Singing
(C) Making a noise
(D) Playing

9. Choose the correct pair of antonyms to fill in the blanks of the following sentence.

___ coffee will get ___ soon.
(A) Cold, cool (B) Hot, cold
(C) Hot, cool (D) Hot, hotter

10. What is the synonym of the underlined word in the following sentence.

We should always <u>respect</u> our elders.
(A) Honour (B) Repeat
(C) Acceptance (D) Listen

11. Identify the correct option with punctuation and capitalization for the following sentence.

The Republic day of India is celebrated _____.
(A) On, January 26
(B) On January, 26
(C) On January 26
(D) On, January, 26

12. Arrange the following shuffled words in a proper sequence.

Class/ student/ am/ two/ I/ the/ of
(A) I am class two of the student.
(B) Class two of the student I am
(C) The student I am of class two.
(D) I am the student of class two.

13. There are some words in English dictionary which are homophones to each other. What is the correct spelling of a number which comes after one and before three?
(A) To (B) Too
(C) Two (D) Tau

14. Identify the collocation in the following sentence.

At the ATM we need to key in our PIN to withdraw the money.
(A) To key in our PIN
(B) ATM PIN
(C) Withdraw the money
(D) We need to

15. Fill in the blank with the appropriate contraction.

My father is very fond of travelling. Nowadays, __ in the eastern part of India.
(A) They're (B) I'm
(C) He's (D) It's

16. Choose the correct option.
(A) A umbrella
(B) An umbrella
(C) The umbrella
(D) No article would be used.

17. Fill in the blank with suitable conjunction.

Saba passed her exams ___ she studied well.

(A) But (B) Hence
(C) Therefore (D) Because

18. Observe the image and answer the following question.

Where are the kids going?

(A) They are going in the school
(B) They are going at the school
(C) They are going on the school
(D) They are going to the school

19. Fill in the blank with suitable adverb.

Ramya __ learned the table and raised her hand in the class.

(A) Keenly (B) Quickly
(C) Easily (D) Well

20. Select the correct word to describe the picture.

(A) Read (B) Write
(C) Laugh (D) Eat

21. Identify the adjective.

I like painting and drawings. Yesterday, I made a drawing of beautiful rose.

(A) Drawing (B) Beautiful
(C) Rose (D) Yesterday

22. Complete the following sentence with appropriate pronoun.

My name is Anushka. I love to spend time with my mother. ____went to watch a movie together, yesterday.

(A) I (B) We
(C) You (D) She

23. Identify the countable noun from the following.

(A) Stars (B) Air
(C) Sun (D) Water

READING

Read the following story carefully and answer the questions from 24 to 26.

A farmer had a goose. That goose laid a beautiful golden egg daily. They used to sell that golden egg and earn lots of money. One day the farmer thought, 'why should I wait for one egg every day, I should cut the stomach of the goose and take out all the eggs.' That brainless farmer cut the abdomen of the goose to take out all the eggs at once, but when he opened the stomach he found nothing but blood.

24. What is the colour of the egg laid by the goose?
(A) White (B) Golden
(C) Red (D) Yellow

25. What did farmer get when he cut the stomach of goose?
(A) Eggs (B) Grams
(C) Blood (D) Bones

26. What did the farmer do with the egg?
(A) Eat it (B) Boil it
(C) Throw it (D) Sell it

SPOKEN AND WRITTEN EXPRESSIONS

27. Chetna: Anamika! Please have a seat.
Anamika: ___
(A) Thank you, Chetna.
(B) It's my pleasure, Chetna.
(C) Get lost, Chetna
(D) I am not your friend Chetna.

28. Choose the correct option which is suitable to complete the sense of the first sentence.
1: My mother was cooking a vegetable soup for me.
2: ?
(A) There were lots of bowls in the kitchen.
(B) There were many chopped vegetables on the kitchen slab.
(C) There were many plates in the kitchen.
(D) There were many spices on the kitchen slab.

29. Choose the correctly punctuated sentence.
(A) The Independence Day of India is celebrated on August 15.
(B) The Independence Day of India, is celebrated on, August 15
(C) The Independence Day of India is celebrated on August, 15
(D) The Independence Day! of India is celebrated on August 15

30. Fill in the blank with proper punctuation mark in the following passage.
Hello Rohan _(i)_ I am your classmate _(ii)_ Vikram_(iii)_ May I borrow your English notes_(iv)_

	(i)	(ii)	(iii)	(iv)
(A)	!	,	.	?
(B)	?	.	!	?
(C)	.	?	!	!
(D)	!	;	?	.

ACHIEVERS SECTION

31. Fill the following blanks with the proper prepositions.
Mohita was going __ Delhi. Her car was running __ the road of highway.
(A) in, on (B) to, at
(C) to, on (D) in, with

32. Identify the verb.

In a cricket match the bowler threw a very fast ball.

(A) Thrown (B) Bowler

(C) Fast (D) Match

33. Fill in the blanks with suitable adjectives.

Shashank, ___ brother and ___ cat were running towards the park.

(A) her, her (B) his, their

(C) her, his (D) his, his

34. Fill in the blanks with suitable articles.

I live in __ small town with my family. Here, we live in __ flat. __ flat is at __ top floor of the building.

(A) an, a, the, a (B) a, a, the, the

(C) a, the, an, a (D) the, a, the, a

35. The quick brown fox jumped over the lazy dog.

Identify the adjective(s).

(A) Quick brown fox

(B) Fox, dog

(C) Quick, brown, lazy

(D) Over

Hints and Solutions

INTERNATIONAL MATHEMATICS OLYMPIAD (IMO)

MOCK TEST PAPER – 1

ANSWERS									
1. (A)	2. (D)	3. (B)	4. (C)	5. (D)	6. (C)	7. (B)	8. (D)	9. (C)	10. (B)
11. (B)	12. (C)	13. (C)	14. (A)	15. (A)	16. (A)	17. (B)	18. (C)	19. (C)	20. (C)
21. (C)	22. (C)	23. (B)	24. (C)	25. (C)	26. (A)	27. (C)	28. (B)	29. (A)	30. (C)
31. (C)	32. (C)	33. (A)	34. (B)	35. (B)					

1. (A) The numbers are increasing in increment of 10, 15, 20 and 25. So the missing number is 60 + 25 = 85.

2. (D) Number of straight lines in the figure is 8.

5. (D) The pattern is to have outside figure with four sides and inside figure with five sides.

7. (B) Code for SET is TES.

8. (D) All other figures are divided into three parts while option (D) figure is divided into four parts.

9. (C) There are six stairs between 5th and 12th stair, 5, 6, 7, 8, 9, 10, 11, 12. Counting the numbers between 5 and 12 we get the answer.

10. (B) Remaining three figures have middle strip as blank and shaded portion outside.

12. (C) In this questions, $8 \times 7 = 56$, 29 more than 56 is $56 - 29 = 27$.

13. (C) Number of bottles each friend gets $= 36 \div 6 = 6$

14. (A) Leap year happens after every four years. Instead of 365 days in a year there are 366 days in the leap year. One day is increased in February, so there are 29 days in February.

15. (A) The given solid has 2 triangular faces.

16. (A) Beaker C holds maximum amount of water i.e. 25 litres.

17. (B) The temperature shown by the thermometer is 35° C.

19. (C) She bought a toy car, a story book and a water bottle as their total cost amounts to ₹ 80.

20. (C) The most popular choice is Chocolate.

21. (C) The number of sisters that Ekta has is $25 \div 5 = 5$

22. (C) Rice left with her is $1000 - (150 + 200) = 650$ g

23. (B) Price of shoes is ₹ 182 + ₹ 118 = ₹ 300. So the total amount that she has to pay is ₹ 182 + ₹ 150 + ₹ 300 = ₹ 632

24.(C) Varsha started practice earliest.

25. (C) The number of books sold in January is $9 \times 2 = 18$

26. (A) No. of triangles she needs is 6.

27. (C) Pinky, Anu and Lalli are holding objects with odd number.

28. (B) Height of Maria's plant is 20 cm + 6 cm = 26 cm

29. (A) Total number of pages is $12 \times 40 = 480$

30. (C) Kanak collected 12 stamps more than Anisha. So, she had $28 + 12 = 40$ stamps. So, both of them collected $28 + 40 = 68$ stamps.

32. (C) The temperature is dropping by 5 degrees each.

33. (A) Paint she bought is $4 \times 2 = 8$ *l*

34. (B) Total mass of 4 bananas is $140 \times 4 = 560$ g. Total mass of both fruits is 860 g. So, mass of the bunch of strawberries is $860 - 560 = 300$ g

35. (B) Cost of cheaper watch is ₹ 100 ÷ ₹ 5 = ₹ 20

MOCK TEST PAPER – 2

ANSWERS									
1. (B)	2. (B)	3. (B)	4. (D)	5. (C)	6. (D)	7. (A)	8. (B)	9. (A)	10. (C)
11. (B)	12. (B)	13. (A)	14. (B)	15. (A)	16. (B)	17. (A)	18. (C)	19. (B)	20. (C)
21. (C)	22. (B)	23. (B)	24. (A)	25. (B)	26. (B)	27. (A)	28. (C)	29. (B)	30. (B)
31. (D)	32. (A)	33. (A)	34. (A)	35. (A)					

1. (B) All figures are divided in two parts, while the figure given in option (B) is divided in three parts.

2. (B) Bead R is at the third position from the top.

6. (D) Length of key is 6 – 2 = 4

11. (B) Number of hot dogs sold on Wednesday was 20.

12. (B) Money they save altogether was ₹ 300 – ₹ 160 = ₹ 140

15. (A) The mat costs ₹ 46.20

17. (A) Option (A) can be put together to form a square.

18. (C) Option (C) has the least value. As 50 divided by 5 is 10.

19. (B) In this question, 4 × 6 is 24 and 3 + 3 + 3 is 9, so 24 – 9 = 15

20. (C) 30 + 8 = 38

21. (C) Money she has now is ₹ 180 + ₹ 20 + ₹ 100 = ₹ 300

23. (B) Each bag weighs 120 ÷ 10 = 12 kg

25. (B) No. of pages left are 162 – 36 = 126

26. (B) Temperature in Jammu is 13 – 4 = 9°C

29. (B) Monika's birthday is on 17th October.

30. (B) Total cost of box is 12 × ₹ 10 = ₹ 120

31. (D) The meeting will end at 1 : 15.

32. (A) Weight of an apple is 350 – 100 = 250 g

33. (A) Total amount he spent is ₹ 50 + ₹ 70 + ₹ 45 = ₹ 165

34. (A) Mukul bought 7 boxes which has 12 pencils each so total pencils with him are 7 × 12 = 84. Pencils he gave to his sister are 20. Pencils left with him are 84 – 20 = 64

35. (A) The room temperature is 20 – 5 = 15° C

NATIONAL SCIENCE OLYMPIAD (NSO)

MOCK TEST PAPER – 1

ANSWERS									
1. (A)	2. (C)	3. (B)	4. (A)	5. (D)	6. (A)	7. (C)	8. (B)	9. (B)	10. (C)
11. (B)	12. (D)	13. (D)	14. (A)	15. (C)	16. (D)	17. (B)	18. (A)	19. (D)	20. (C)
21. (B)	22. (A)	23. (D)	24. (D)	25. (D)	26. (A)	27. (C)	28. (D)	29. (D)	30. (C)
31. (D)	32. (D)	33. (B)	34. (D)	35. (A)					

1. (A) The time shown in the clock is 2:40. It is half an hour later i.e. 30 minutes later to 2:10.

2. (C) In this image the figure is moving clockwise, first it was pointing towards up left, then up right, and then down left is shown. So the missing part should be down right

3. (B) Hoof is end portion of legs of horse, so the end portion of hand/ leg of cat, which is paw should be given.

4. (A) She is 12th from bottom so there are 12 kids and she is 16th from top so there are 16 kids, so adding up and excluding one since her position is counted twice,
$12 + 16 - 1 = 27$ students

5. (D) In the given set of numbers all the numbers are odd and non-divisible except 9 and 15. 9 and 15 are divisible numbers.

6. (A) In the given image sugarcane is shown. The juice from it is used to make sugar.

7. (C) Mint and spinach are leafy parts of the plant. So these are obtained from leaves.

8. (B) Plants with weak stem that cannot stand upright and spread on the ground are called creepers. Both watermelon and bottle gourds are creepers. Some more creepers are pumpkin, sweet potato.

9. (B) Animals that are friendly and could live at home are called domestic animals. So, goat, dog and cow are domestic animals. Some other examples are cat, sheep.

10. (C) Leather is made up of skin.

11. (B) Tongue helps us to speak.

12. (D) The heart pumps blood in our body. It helps in transferring oxygen and nutrition in the body.

13. (D) All are unhealthy food except option D which is full of nutrition. Eating chapatis, green vegetables and *dals* makes us healthy.

14. (A) In Indian meals pickles are very common. Pickling is a method of preserving the food by using oil and salt. Various types of pickles include that of mango, lemon, carrot.

15. (C) Wool is obtained from sheep (animal) whereas cotton plant (plant) gives us cotton.

16. (D) Stethoscope is an instrument used by doctors to hear heart sounds. A doctor wears one part of it in his ears whereas the other is kept on the chest of the patient to hear heart sounds.

18. (A) Tailor sews and mends our clothes and uses sewing tools like thread, buttons, scissors, sewing machine, safety pin.

19. (D) We should not spit on the road to keep the roads clean. We should cross the road through zebra crossing for safety. We should not run in the middle of the road as the vehicles might hurt you.

20. (C) Traffic signals on roads have three lights: red, yellow and green. The red signifies stop, the yellow signifies that we should wait or go slow and the green light signifies that we should go.

21. (B) The sun rises from East and sets in West, so in the morning when we are facing the sun, we are facing East. Behind East is West and on right side is South and left side is North.

22. (A) Bullock cart is a vehicle pulled by bullocks and it is used for carrying people and goods.

23. (D) A place is identified by its Postal Index Number (PIN). This number helps postal department to exactly locate the place based on state, district, post office code etc. In India this is a six digit number where first two digit reflects a region (State).

24.(D) Diamond is hardest substance on the earth. Gold, platinum, diamond are precious minerals and these are used for making of jewellery.

25. (D) Wells, hand pumps, tube wells are used to obtain groundwater.

26. (A) The Earth moves around its axis which causes day and night. This is called rotation. The earth also moves around the Sun which

causes seasons (Winter, Summer, Rain and Autumn) and this movement is called revolution.

27. (C) Moon does not have light of its own. Moon receives light from Sun. It also does not have air.

28. (D) Earth is our planet. We live on the earth, it has air, water and supports life.

29. (D) All are good habits while wiping your nose with curtains as shown in option D is a bad habit. It makes your home dirty.

30. (C) Biting your nail is a bad habit. It makes you look bad in front of others and it can make you fall ill because harmful bacteria gets accumulated in the nail and skin space and if you bit the nails those may get transferred to your body through the mouth.

32. (D) All are correct. You should take help of your parents to understand the sign boards clearly.

33. (B) The Moon doesn't emit (give off) light itself, the 'moonlight' we see is actually the Sun's light reflected off the lunar surface. So, as the Moon orbits the Earth, the Sun lights up different parts of it, making it seem as if the Moon is changing shape. Till first 15 days it seems to grow. On 15th day it becomes full moon. After full moon the size of moon seems to start decreasing. After 15 days it disappears, and that night is called as dark moon.

34. (D) ATM (Automated teller machine) is used to withdraw money. As a good citizen we should wait for our turn. The person who is operating the machine should hide his password and another person should not try to read his password. It is a crime as well as bad manner.

35. (A) Cotton is obtained from fruits, jute is obtained from stem, wool is obtained from hair of animals like sheep and silk is obtained from cocoon of silkworm.

MOCK TEST PAPER – 2

ANSWERS									
1. (A)	2. (B)	3. (A)	4. (D)	5. (C)	6. (A)	7. (B)	8. (B)	9. (A)	10. (B)
11. (B)	12. (C)	13. (A)	14. (B)	15. (A)	16. (D)	17. (C)	18. (A)	19. (C)	20. (B)
21. (A)	22. (B)	23. (C)	24. (D)	25. (A)	26. (C)	27. (D)	28. (B)	29. (A)	30. (C)
31. (D)	32. (A)	33. (D)	34. (C)	35. (C)					

1. (A) Pizza has a circular shape. When it is divided into pieces, then each piece has a triangular shape.

3. (A) Each alphabet gets a number from 1 to 26. For example, A is 1, B is 2, C is 3 and so on till Z which is 26. S is 19th alphabet, A is 1st alphabet, D is 4th alphabet. So SAD is 1914.

5. (C) Each number in the series is double of previous one. For example, 6 is double of 3, 12 is double of 6, 24 is double of 12, so the next number should be 48 which is double of 24.

6. (A) Bicycle is a slow-moving vehicle and is used on land. So, it is an example of slow land transport.

7. (B) Submarine is the underwater mode of transport as it gets submerged into the water.

8. (B) The body surrounding the Earth (our planet) is called its satellite. Earth has one natural satellite i.e. Moon.

9. (A) During sunrise the sun is brighter than sunset. The birds are active and they are going to fetch food.

10. (B) Sun is a star which looks like a huge fire ball. We get heat and light from the Sun.

11. (B) Solar system contains 8 planets and sun.

12.(C) Diamond is the hardest substance. It is so hard that it is used to cut hard materials.

13. (A) Water conservation or water saving is to use the same water for multiple works to avoid its wastage. Water pollution is polluting the water through garbage and other dirty things. Water harvesting is to store the water.

14. (B) The person who cannot speak and hear uses sign language to communicate. There are various symbols which are made by gesture of hand that helps those persons to communicate.

15. (A) In video calling both persons on each side of communication can see and hear each other

even though they are at different places.

16. (D) Indoor games are the ones which are played inside. While outdoor games are played in gardens, lawns. Badminton is an outdoor game.

17. (C) In such cases, you should run for help and call an adult to help your friend. First aid must be given to provide some help in healing the wounds.

18. (A) An army man or a soldier helps to protect our country from enemies. They have guns, cannon to protect the country.

19. (C) A potter makes various things like pots, dishes, mugs, vases. using mud, clay, water. He has a potter wheel that helps him in making such items.

20.(B) Bucket is kept in bathroom, which is a place to take bath.

21. (A) Igloo is a dome shaped house made in cold places where there is snow. It is made up of snow and is built by the people living in snow, who are called eskimo.

22. (B) Breakfast should be the heaviest meal since during the day you work out a lot, so it is digested easily. Dinner should be the lightest since after dinner, we go to sleep and there is no activity and so digestion process is slow.

23. (C) These foods are body-building foods as they help us to grow.

24. (D) The structure of human body is made up of bones and muscles. Bones provide a fixed shape to our body and with the help of muscles the bones move and we are able to perform various actions.

25. (A) Skeleton is frame of our body.

26. (C) Cow's baby is called calf and Kangaroo's baby is called Joeys.

28. (B) When young plants grow to adult stage, then they start flowering. So adult plants have flowers while the young plants do not have flowers.

29. (A) Leaves help the plants to make their food. So if the plants will not have leaves, they will not be able to make their food.

30. (C) Woods are obtained from pine trees. These are used in making various items like furniture, windows, frames, panelling, floors and roofing.

31. (D) The given plants are rose and hibiscus. Both plants are shrubs, so their stems are woody. The flowering plants always give seeds.

32.(A) The image shows a sweater (1) which is made up of wool that is obtained from sheep. The second image shows a bag which is made up of leather that obtained from skin of dead animals like crocodile. Third image shows a saree made up of silk that is obtained from silk worm.

33. (D) You can't see colours if you are blindfolded so you cannot differentiate between papers with different colours but you can taste the juice and smell the flowers even if you are blindfolded since tongue is used to taste and nose is used to smell.

34. (C) Fruits are Q, R is milk, P is meat.

35. (C) Clothes are made from yarn using looms, the process of manufacturing clothes is called as weaving.

NATIONAL CYBER OLYMPIAD (NCO)

MOCK TEST PAPER – 1

ANSWERS									
1. (C)	2. (B)	3. (B)	4. (C)	5. (B)	6. (D)	7. (A)	8. (C)	9. (D)	10. (B)
11. (A)	12. (C)	13. (B)	14. (B)	15. (B)	16. (A)	17. (C)	18. (B)	19. (D)	20. (C)
21. (D)	22. (B)	23. (C)	24. (D)	25. (A)	26. (B)	27. (D)	28. (D)	29. (A)	30. (B)
31. (D)	32. (C)	33. (B)	34. (C)	35. (A)					

1. (C) 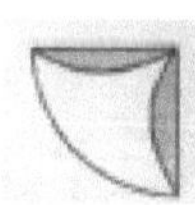

2. (B) Here, 5 groups of 3 butterflies can be formed from the given figures.

3. (B) First figure when joined with second figure will make a complete figure.

4. (C) Phone is used for calling but here phone is called television. So, television is used for calling.

6. (D) Speakers. Output device provides information.

7. (A) Folder

8. (C) Booting

9. (D) Restart

10. (B) ALU. It stands for Arithmetic Logic Unit.

11. (A) Username

12. (C) Data cable

13. (B)  - Microphone. Option (A) is speaker, option (C) is monitor, option (D) is web camera.

14. (B) Web camera

15. (B) Password

16. (A) Navigation keys

17. (C) It displays list of commands on the screen.

18. (B) Shift key

19. (D) It appears on the bottom left of the monitor.
20. (C) Shopping Malls– Billing
21. (D) CPU (Central Processing Unit)
22. (B) Optical mouse
23. (C) Cut
24. (D) IPO stands for Input Process Output.
25. (A) App stands for application.
26. (B)
27. (D) while others are tools in MS Paint.
28. (D) All of these. Option (A) is Facebook, option (B) is Instagram and option (C) is Twitter.
29. (A) SCROLL WHEEL and it is found on mouse.
30. (B) Uninterrupted Power Supply
31. (D) Arrow keys
32. (C) Drag and drop
33. (B) It shows the hard copy of the output. It is a printer.
34. (C) Start
35. (A) A – Text tool

    Turning off the computer – Shut Down

    Processing Unit – CPU

    Device used during power failure – UPS

MOCK TEST PAPER – 2

ANSWERS									
1. (C)	2. (A)	3. (D)	4. (B)	5. (A)	6. (C)	7. (C)	8. (D)	9. (B)	10. (A)
11. (C)	12. (A)	13. (B)	14. (C)	15. (B)	16. (A)	17. (D)	18. (D)	19. (B)	20. (A)
21. (D)	22. (C)	23. (B)	24. (C)	25. (A)	26. (C)	27. (D)	28. (B)	29. (A)	30. (C)
31. (D)	32. (C)	33. (A)	34. (B)	35. (C)					

1. (C) The shaded portion is taken forward to get the second figure.
2. (A) The pattern given in the series is 7 + 5, 12 + 5 ....Hence 32 will complete the series.
3. (D) No. of students = 37. Priya ranked 11th from top that means there are 10 students above her, and she ranked 27th from bottom so there are 26 students below her. So total students are

   10 + 1 + 26 = 37.
5. (A) In the given code, a word is completely reversed. Similarly, the code for 7826 is 6287.

6. (C) UPS (Uninterrupted Power Supply)

7. (C) MHz
8. (D) This is webcam. To capture a video image of the scene in front of it.
9. (B) Supercomputers
10. (A) Taskbar
11. (C) Microphone
12. (A) Tab key
13. (B) Right. This is right click in a Mouse.
14. (C) Joystick
15. (B) Drawing Area
16. (A) Double clicking
17. (D) Spacebar Key
18. (D) Writing story
19. (B) Ctrl and Alt key
20. (A) If you want to erase the letter before the cursor then backspace key is pressed.
21. (D) Since it is not bigger than the desktop.
22. (C) iPhone XS
23. (B) Both statement 1 and 2
24. (C) 
25. (A) Copy
26. (C) 

\+ 

27. (D) Banks- withdrawal of money through ATM
28. (B) Scroll wheel
29. (A) Input process output
30. (C) Colour
31. (D)  - It is used to select a part of a picture.
32. (C) The given word is JOYSTICK. It is used to play games on the computer.
33. (A) Enter key or 

34. (B) Steps to create folder
    1. Right click on desktop.
    2. Click on "New".
    3. Click on " Folder".
    4. Type the name of the folder and press Enter key.
35. (C) Key used to cancel any command action – Esc Key
    Drag and drop – Moves an item on screen
    To activate numeric keypad on keyboard – Num lock
    Small pictures on the desktop screen – Icons

INTERNATIONAL ENGLISH OLYMPIAD (IEO)

MOCK TEST PAPER – 1

ANSWERS									
1. (A)	2. (C)	3. (A)	4. (A)	5. (C)	6. (B)	7. (C)	8. (D)	9. (B)	10. (A)
11. (A)	12. (C)	13. (A)	14. (A)	15. (C)	16. (D)	17. (D)	18. (D)	19. (C)	20. (B)
21. (A)	22. (C)	23. (A)	24. (B)	25. (A)	26. (C)	27. (D)	28. (C)	29. (B)	30. (B)
31. (A)	32. (A)	33. (A)	34. (C)	35. (D)					

1. (A) Common noun never starts with capital letters.
3. (A) Adjectives tell about the nature of the noun.
4. (A) The verb represents the activity of the noun.
5. (C) Adverbs tell us when the action is to be performed.
7. (C) Conjunctions are used to club or attach two sentences.
8. (D) An is used for the word starting from vowel (a, e, i, o, u) and a is used for the word starting from a consonant
9. (B) He + is can be contracted to he's. In contraction pronoun and verb are contracted together.
10. (A) Collocation is the group of two or more words which are commonly used in English.
14. (A) Wise and intelligent are synonyms of each other.
15. (C) Better and worse are antonyms to each other.
18. (D) Domestic animals can be kept as a pet or can be kept in a farm.
19. (C) Gregarious animals are those which do not stay in a herd. Polar bears have solitary life.
22. (C) Past progressive or continuous tense indicates about an action which was happening in the past.
23. (A) Whatever you do in a regular manner comes in the present continuous tense.
26. (C) The colour of the snow is white therefore the ground is white.
27. (D) Semicolon is used to join two different related clauses.
32. (A) Refusal refers to the unacceptance of something
33. (A) Feminine of emperor is empress.
34. (C) It's is contraction of It + is. It is used when we are talking about a definite object.
35. (D) Unscrambling of tub gives us 'but' which is used to show the difference.

MOCK TEST PAPER – 2

ANSWERS									
1. (A)	2. (A)	3. (C)	4. (B)	5. (C)	6. (B)	7. (D)	8. (B)	9. (B)	10. (A)
11. (B)	12. (D)	13. (C)	14. (A)	15. (C)	16. (B)	17. (D)	18. (D)	19. (B)	20. (A)
21. (B)	22. (B)	23. (C)	24. (B)	25. (C)	26. (D)	27. (A)	28. (B)	29. (C)	30. (A)
31. (C)	32. (A)	33. (B)	34. (B)	35. (C)					

1. (A) Do and does are the helping verbs of the present indefinite tense.
2. (A) First form of the verb is used in the case of universal facts.
3. (C) Sachin Tendulkar is alive so it is a present tense.
4. (B) Tomorrow indicates that the sentence is future indefinite. Shall/ Will are the helping verbs of future indefinite. With I and We, shall is used as helping verb.
5. (C) Elephant, horse and deer are herbivores while lion is carnivore. Dogs and cats are omnivores (Eat both plants and animals).
6. (B) Colt is the male baby of a horse and filly is a female baby of the horse. A baby of cow is called as calf.
9. (B) Hot and cold are antonyms of each other.
10. (A) Respect and honour have the same meaning.
13. (C) One, two, three… and so on.
14. (A) Collocation is the group of two or more words which are commonly used in English.
15. (C) He + is can be contracted to he's. In contraction pronoun and verb are contracted together.
16. (B) With an object starting with a vowel, the article 'an' is used.
17. (D) Conjunctions are used to join the sentence.
18. (D) When someone and something is moving towards another thing or place, 'to' preposition is used.
19. (B) Most of the adverbs ends with '-ly'. In the given sentence Ramya raised her hand in the class so she has to learn table fast and quick.
20. (A) The girl is reading a book in the given picture.
21. (B) Adjective tells about the nature of the noun.
22. (B) We is used as the pronoun for two or more persons.
23. (C) Sun is countable noun because there is one sun in the whole universe. Stars, air and water are uncountable because they can not be counted on the fingertips.
27. (A) If someone offers us something, we should say thank you.

28. (B) As mother is cooking vegetable soup, lots of chopped vegetables are required.

30. (A) When we address someone, exclamatory mark is used. While introducing someone, coma is used before name and at the completion of introduction full stop is used. The seconds part of the sentence is seeking of permission so question mark will be used.

32. (A) Throwing is an activity.

33. (B) Shashank is a boy so his is used to address his brother and he and his brother has a cat so their is used to address the cat.

35. (C) Quick, brown and lazy are the descriptive adjectives.

9 789357 942270

Printed by Libri Plureos GmbH in Hamburg, Germany